The WAC Journal

Writing Across the Curriculum
Volume 26
2015

© 2015 Clemson University
Printed on acid-free paper in the USA
ISSN: 1544-4929

Editor

Roy Andrews

Managing Editor

Lea Anna Cardwell, Clemson University

Associate Editors

David Blakesley, Clemson University
Michael LeMahieu, Clemson University

Editorial Board

Art Young, Clemson University
Neal Lerner, Northeastern University
Carol Rutz, Carleton College
Meg Petersen, Plymouth State University
Terry Myers Zawacki, George Mason Univ.

Review Board

Jacob S. Blumner, Univ of Michigan, Flint
Patricia Donahue, Lafayette College
John Eliason, Gonzaga University
Michael LeMahieu, Clemson University
Neal Lerner, Northeastern University
Meg Petersen, Plymouth State University
Mya Poe, Northeastern University
Carol Rutz, Carleton College
Joanna Wolfe, University of Louisville
Terry Myers Zawacki, George Mason Univ.
David Zehr, Plymouth State University

Subscription Information

The WAC Journal
Parlor Press
3015 Brackenberry Drive
Anderson SC 29621
wacjournal@parlorpress.com
parlorpress.com/wacjournal
Rates: 1 year: $25; 3 years: $65; 5 years: $95.

Submissions

The editorial board of *The WAC Journal* seeks WAC-related articles from across the country. Our national review board welcomes inquiries, proposals, and 3,000 to 6,000 word articles on WAC-related topics, including the following: WAC Techniques and Applications; WAC Program Strategies; WAC and WID; WAC and Writing Centers; Interviews and Reviews. Proposals and articles outside these categories will also be considered. Any discipline-standard documentation style (MLA, APA, etc.) is acceptable, but please follow such guidelines carefully. Submissions are managed initially via Submittable (https://parlorpress.submittable.com/submit) and then via email. For general inquiries, contact Lea Anna Cardwell, the managing editor, via email (wacjournal@parlorpress.com). The WAC Journal is an open-access, blind, peer-viewed journal published annually by Clemson University, Parlor Press, and the WAC Clearinghouse. It is available in print through Parlor Press and online in open-access format at the WAC Clearinghouse. *The WAC Journal* is peer-reviewed. It is published annually by Clemson University, Parlor Press, and the WAC Clearinghouse.

Subscriptions

The WAC Journal is published annually in print by Parlor Press and Clemson University. Digital copies of the journal are simultaneously published at The WAC Clearinghouse in PDF format for free download. Print subscriptions support the ongoing publication of the journal and make it possible to offer digital copies as open access. Subscription rates: One year: $25; Three years: $65; Five years: $95. You can subscribe to The WAC Journal and pay securely by credit card or PayPal at the Parlor Press website: http://www.parlorpress.com/wacjournal. Or you can send your name, email address, and mailing address along with a check (payable to Parlor Press) to Parlor Press, 3015 Brackenberry Drive, Anderson SC 29621. Email: sales@parlorpress.com

Reproduction of material from this publication, with acknowledgement of the source, is hereby authorized for educational use in non-profit organizations.

The WAC Journal
Volume 26, 2015

Contents

What Do WAC Directors Need to Know about "Coverage"?　　　7
ERIKA SCHEURER

An Affordance Approach to WAC Development and Sustainability　　22
SHERRY LEE LINKON AND MATTHEW PAVESICH

"Emphasizing Similarity" but Not "Eliding Difference":
Exploring Sub-Disciplinary Differences as a Way to Teach Genre Flexibly　　36
KATHERINE L. SCHAEFER

Cross-Curricular Consulting: How WAC Experts Can Practice Adult
Learning Theory to Build Relationships with Disciplinary Faculty　　56
DENISE ANN VRCHOTA

At the Commencement of an Archive: The National Census of Writing
and the State of Writing Across the Curriculum　　76
CAITLIN CORNELL HOLMES

Do You Believe in Good Academic Writing?　　100
MARY HEDENGREN

The Man Behind the WAC Clearinghouse: Mike Palmquist　　105
CAROL RUTZ

Contributors　　113

What Do WAC Directors Need to Know about "Coverage"?

ERIKA SCHEURER

I frequently hear the following comment from faculty colleagues across the disciplines: "I can't possibly add more attention to writing in my course because I already have too much I need to cover. If I do more with writing, I'll have to drop half the nineteenth century" (or number theory or the function of the small intestine). This statement is usually made in a frustrated, even overwhelmed, tone of voice.

They are not the only ones who are frustrated. My goal as a WAC director, after all, is to help faculty members learn to use writing as a *means* of "covering" material, not to view it in opposition to coverage. Yet despite the fact that the idea of "writing as a means of coverage" is indeed covered in our five-day WAC seminar, faculty members often still use the same language of "coverage" to forestall more attention to writing. It is as if their courses are finite vessels that can hold only so much content. Writing is seen as yet more liquid added to the vessel, displacing existing content and causing the whole thing to overflow into a mess.

Over my six years as WAC director at a medium-size private comprehensive university, I have come to realize that whether I like it or not, "coverage" is the language faculty members speak. In order to understand this language better, I conducted research on the concept of coverage based on pedagogical scholarship and on a survey of faculty members conducted in November 2013. What I have learned about faculty attitudes towards coverage has complicated my thinking on the topic and led me to more effective and satisfying conversations with my colleagues across the disciplines.

But First, What about "Uncoverage"?

The idea of "coverage" has certainly not gone without critique. We could reach back to John Dewey's *Experience and Education,* where he rejects the concept that static knowledge of content, rather than its connection to the student's *experience* of that content, serves as the end of education. Later, in a 1965 article, "The Idea of Coverage in the Teaching of Literature," George H. Henry, professor of education at the University of Delaware, scathingly critiques the coverage approach to the teaching of high school literature surveys. Looking at coverage "in light of the present explosion of knowledge," Henry dramatically points out the impossibility of covering increasing amounts of classic literature in the same limited span of time, exclaiming,

> Imagine what another thirty years will bring! How can the method of coverage ever cope with it all? Will we merely compress and speed-up, cut snippets from more works for students to touch with the tip of the tongue to get a taste. Our courses are fast becoming a package of samplers. (476)

Applying cognitive psychology to teaching, Henry advocates for an exploratory, concept-development method for teaching literature to replace "the additive, time-centered, item-strewn method of coverage" (477). He notes, "a concept is best developed slowly and through the progressive development of meaning in time and must be arrived at through discovery" (479). His non-coverage-based literature survey is organized by thematic strands, not chronology, and aims to interrogate key questions. He argues that in doing away with what he calls the "stuffage" method, one third of the literature currently covered in surveys could be dropped "and we would do our task much better" (481). Interestingly, one element of doing the task better includes clearing up room for more attention to student writing.

The essential elements of Henry's critique and solution to the problem of coverage reappear decades later in more current pedagogical scholarship. The concept of "uncoverage"—coined by Grant Wiggins and Jay McTighe (2005)—describes a push to free survey courses of the coverage model, replacing it with thematic and skill-based courses designed to teach students what practitioners in a field value and how they think. Of those applying the concept of "uncoverage" to pedagogy in their fields, E. Shelley Reid (introduction to composition theory and pedagogy) and Lendol Calder (the American history survey) do so most thoroughly.

Both present the problem of having too much information to cover in too little time based on their personal experiences, then point to the larger assumptions about teaching and learning embedded in the idea of coverage: "Everywhere, the mystique of coverage is abating. Teachers no longer believe they can cover everything of importance..." (Calder 1359). Calder, like Henry, draws on cognitive psychology in launching his critique of the coverage model, referencing "what Sam Wineburg calls the 'attic theory' of cognition"—that we collect information and store it away for later (1361). This is not how the mind works and, argues Calder, it actually leads to less learning:

> The problem with defenders of traditional surveys, then, is not that they care about facts too much but that they do not care about facts enough to inquire into the nature of how people learn them. Built on wobbly, lay theories of human cognition, coverage-oriented surveys must share the blame for Americans' deplorable ignorance of history. (1362)

Likewise, Reid critiques the pervasive, "default-nature of coverage pedagogy" (16), advocating for an approach similar to that currently employed for first-year writing for graduate composition theory students:

> As we develop and improve courses for teachers of college composition, then, I argue that we need—very deliberately, publicly, and collectively—to focus on *uncoverage,* to emphasize discoveries that lead to long-term learning over immediate competencies. That is, we need to conceive of the pedagogy course at its foundation in the way that we now conceive of first-year writing: as an intellectual engagement rather than an inoculation, as practice in a way of encountering the world rather than mastery of skills or facts, as preparation for a lifetime of *thinking like a teacher.*" (16)

Despite their completely different courses and students—Calder teaches the undergraduate history survey as a general requirement course; Reid teaches a graduate-level pedagogy course for future composition teachers—these scholars arrive at similar solutions to the coverage problem. Both replace their traditional surveys with problem- or issue-driven courses aimed at helping students to think and act like practitioners in their fields. Interestingly, with the focus on the exploration of disciplinary problems rather than on facts and solutions, both include a focus on writing to learn pedagogy as well.

What Faculty Members Say

Neither Henry, Reid, nor Calder pretend that switching from a coverage model to "uncoverage" is easy.[1] Indeed, Henry refers to the time that he "traumatically broke with coverage" (481). In order to work with the faculty members at my university, I needed to better understand what professional and emotional connections they feel towards the concept of coverage. What obstacles stand in the way of their adopting more of an "uncoverage" pedagogical approach, presumably one that would allow for more attention to writing?

Also, the scholars I have cited who have published on "uncoverage" are tenured faculty members in the humanities and education. What influence does the faculty member's academic discipline and status within the academy have on views of coverage? Did faculty members who completed our five-day WAC seminar approach coverage differently from faculty members who have not?[2] As I work with hundreds of faculty colleagues in over thirty diverse disciplines, before I could reply to the "coverage" argument for not drawing in more support of writing into courses, I needed to know more about how different subsets of the faculty viewed coverage.

To this end, in the Fall semester of 2013 I developed and administered a campus-wide anonymous survey to which I invited faculty members to respond. The survey included the following questions:

- In connection to your teaching, what does the term "coverage" mean to you?
- Compared to all of your other goals as an instructor, how important is achieving coverage to you in your teaching? (a scale of "extremely important" to "not at all important") Why?
- What primarily influences your approach to coverage in your teaching? Rank the following from 1 to 5, with 1 as most influential: My own teaching goals, Departmental expectations, School/college expectations, Expectations of a larger accrediting body, Other.
- What is your primary means of achieving coverage? Rank the following options with "1" as the means you use the most: Giving lectures in class, Assigning students to view lectures online outside of class, Assigning reading, Assigning Writing, Class discussions, Other.
- Please describe up to three of the most significant challenges to your achieving coverage of course material in your classes.
- Has your attitude about the importance of coverage changed over the course of your teaching career? Yes/No. Please explain.
- Have your methods of achieving coverage changed over the course of your teaching career? Yes/no. Please explain.
- What else would you like to say about coverage that has not been addressed in the above questions?

Of approximately 493 full-time and 383 adjunct faculty members overall, 122 faculty members responded to the survey, with varying response rates for individual questions. The demographic breakdown of the respondents is as follows:

Table 1. Academic discipline.

Arts and Humanities	60 (English: 19; theology: 12)
STEM disciplines	27
Social Sciences	17
College of Business	12
Education	4
Law	1
Not indicated	2

Table 2. Gender.

Female	73
Male	49

Table 3. Faculty status.

Adjunct	23
Limited-term	1
Clinical	5
Tenured	68
Tenure-track	25

Table 4. Participation in five-day WAC seminar.

Yes ("WAC faculty")	60
No	62

Although the percentage of faculty members who took the survey is not high, their diverse makeup and rich qualitative responses have yielded a wellspring of thought-provoking information. My interpretation of both the quantitative and qualitative elements of the survey has led me to the following insights.

Insight #1: Faculty members define coverage differently and, though the majority of faculty members highly value coverage as a course goal, they value it for different reasons. So when one faculty member uses the word "coverage" it may have entirely different valences of meaning from when another faculty member uses the word.

Of 92 comments in which faculty members define coverage, 59 do so strictly in terms of material conveyed to students. For some, the concept is fairly straightforward: "It means covering the period 1600 to 1877 in U.S. History." This corresponds with the definition of coverage critiqued in the "uncoverage" literature. Others feel more conflicted about this definition of coverage:

> To explicitly address or assign a genre or time period or terminology or particular texts that students would be expected to know as an outcome of the course. That is, that I would feel remiss or irresponsible in their not knowing. When I use the word "coverage," though, I'm usually thinking in a reactive way—that I must "cover" X or Y for students to move up a level or because my colleagues would be appalled if my course didn't include X. Coverage feels broad and thin rather than deep. (Still, it exerts a real pressure.)

A number of faculty members—33 of the 92—define coverage in broader ways that include skills as well as material covered:

> For me, coverage is not limited to the disseminating of knowledge/content. It also must include skill development and appreciation of dispositions appropriate to the discipline. Facts are important, but with today's explosion of knowledge and technology, I think it is more important to learn how to appropriate this knowledge in meaningful and productive ways.

And

> I think it's also possible to think of "coverage" not as a set list of texts or movements (e.g.[,] "we have to cover Twain!") but as a range of APPROACHES to texts (and to writing about texts).

Thus, while some faculty members think of coverage in the traditional sense of conveying information to students, others employ more of an "uncoverage" approach or see coverage as including skills and dispositions as well as informational content.

No matter how they define coverage, faculty members overwhelmingly value it as a course goal. Compared to their other goals as instructors, 30 faculty members surveyed identify achieving coverage as "extremely important;" 50 as "very important;" 19 as "neither important nor unimportant"; 2 as "very unimportant;" and zero chose "not at all important." WAC faculty members valued coverage as a course goal equally as much as other faculty members, with 80% finding it either extremely or very important.

The reasons faculty members value coverage vary, however. For some, the students' need for information is the primary reason they value coverage. For example, a faculty member from philosophy notes that students need the information covered "to live a meaningful life." Other faculty members, mostly in the humanities, cite departmental expectations of what needs to be covered in certain courses (especially core general requirement courses). They mention the scaffolding of knowledge in curricula: when courses serve as prerequisites for higher-level courses, they must cover certain material.

Faculty members also cite student expectations for what is covered (a "contract" with students) and refer to a sense of responsibility, conscience, moral obligation, and the integrity of the discipline. Finally, particularly in disciplines such as business, social work, STEM, and education, faculty members mention the requirements of states, accrediting bodies, and licensure boards. Other significant outside influences are employers and the expectations students will face in the workplace. Of students who will become engineers, one faculty member comments that "People can die" if information is not covered.

When we work with faculty members, then, it is important for us to recognize that, while most highly value coverage as a course goal, they define coverage differently and value it for different reasons. While not necessarily surprising, the fact that that faculty members, not only across disciplines but also within them, may hold vastly diverging ideas about coverage serves to remind WAC directors that one of our first questions when working with faculty members should be, "What do you mean by coverage?" Establishing this baseline is essential before we can move forward in the conversation. These differing reasons for valuing coverage are connected to the constraints and pressures they feel regarding coverage.

Insight #2: Most faculty members cite time and students as significant factors that hinder their ability to cover material. Not all faculty members are free to decide what they do and do not cover, however. Depending on their academic discipline and status, they feel varying constraints and stresses concerning coverage.

Common Constraints

Unsurprisingly, "time" is the single most often-cited challenge to achieving coverage cited by faculty members; after all, lack of time is essentially what makes coverage a "problem." Even back in 1965, Henry bemoans the tyranny of time in a coverage-centered model of education. Discussing an experiment in addressing the concept of "nature" through student engagement in writing and discussion rather than faculty lecture, he mentions a teacher who refused to participate "because she thought it was a waste of time": "'I can teach nature in three days.' Certainly, I can teach it in thirty minutes, too! Notice how time always dominates the concept of 'coverage' in a syllabus" (478).

Asked to list three challenges to achieving coverage, faculty members made 55 references to lack of time (a few faculty members listed "time" for all three):

> TIME! It really challenges: 1, 2, and 3.

> Too much material. The longer I am in the field the more I know and the more I think is important.

> Balancing the pace of the course (recognizing that it takes both time and work for students to "get" something, and doesn't serve anyone well if we move on to the next thing before that happens).

Another challenge presented by students to the faculty's ability to achieve coverage was lack of student motivation and engagement (29 citations):

> 1. Students who have not completed the reading assignments before coming to class 2. Students who are reluctant to participate in class discussions 3. Students who do not attend class regularly.
>
> Student motivation and time spent on the course outside of class. If students do not spend enough time outside of class working through problems and understanding concepts, then we must spend more time in class before we can move on.

Like lack of time, lack of student engagement is not a particularly new problem. We work hard to engage students, but ultimate control of student engagement remains elusive—ask anyone who has ever taught two sections of the exact same course back to back, one with engaged students and the other with indifferent students. Understandably, faculty members find the constraint on coverage presented by lack of student motivation extremely frustrating.

Discipline- and Status-Specific Constraints

While time and student engagement are perceived as challenges to achieving coverage across the board, other challenges appear to be more specific to certain disciplines or levels of faculty status. For example, 33 faculty members listed lack of student preparation as inhibiting their ability to achieve coverage. Because students did not know information or were not able to perform a certain skill, faculty members were not able to cover what they intended.

While student lack of preparation is cited across the disciplines, it is mentioned more frequently by faculty members in the STEM disciplines in which knowledge is carefully scaffolded. Eleven of 27 of STEM faculty members (41%) cite lack of student preparation vs. 13 of 60 (22%) of those in the humanities faculty. Lack of student preparation can set back faculty learning objectives considerably:

> Students who tell me "we never saw that before. . . ." when I try to build on material they should have had.
>
> Inadequate student preparation before Physics classes (math and problem solving skills).

In addition to lack of student engagement and preparation, some faculty members perceive a conflict between student and faculty expectations about coverage. For faculty members working to achieve tenure, the connection between what they cover and student ratings is a source of concern.[3]

> From my experience, students think they learn more when there's more coverage—i.e.[,] they can "see" all the "things they've learned" (facts, knowledge,

etc.), which may influence faculty [members] in providing more coverage/breadth. However, my personal philosophy is that students actually learn more (and become better learners) when there's more depth (and thus less breadth/coverage), even though they don't necessarily realize it. This gets at that nebulous "critical thinking" goal—students don't always realize how much their thinking is improved, [sic] but can fairly easily determine how much their factual knowledge has increased by the end of the course. I think this pressures faculty [members] into focusing more on coverage at the expense of depth, which in my opinion does a disservice to the students, the professors, and the profession. (Now how to combat this . . . that's the real question!)

... [G]iven the heavy emphasis on IDEA scores as a measure of faculty teaching, coverage also must address student satisfaction. Students feel like they've learned something if they memorize long lists of terms and understand what happened when. So in my teaching, I also must cover a clear chronology that covers the time period and geographical area of the course description, and give students the impression that nothing is left out and they know everything they need to know.

Yet, the pressures of student evaluations can work in the opposite direction as well:

I cover less now because of student resistance [to fact-based instruction].

As if the power exerted by time and students over what faculty members can and cannot cover were not enough, the actual learning objectives—what needs to be covered—are not always a matter of faculty choice. In fields such as business, social work, education, and pre-medicine, faculty members mention outside expectations such as those for accreditation, licensure, preparation for the MCAT, etc. Another significant challenge for faculty members in achieving coverage are the expectations—or sometimes, lack of clarity about expectations—of their departments or fields.

Lack of consensus in my department and in my field generally as to the importance of the actual knowledge base of the field (as opposed to skills and practices).

In our department intro class[,] coverage is determined by department decision, and is very strict and exacting, and encompasses a lot of material. It is a strain to maintain coverage in that class.

While for all faculty members surveyed, "my own teaching goals" ranked as by far the primary influence on the approach to coverage (43 faculty members) with departmental expectations a distant second (22 faculty members), for adjunct and limited-term faculty members, departmental expectations are the primary influence (8) with individual goals a close second (7). This finding may correlate to the adjunct faculty's overall higher rating of the importance of coverage as a course goal: compared to 80% of all those surveyed, 95% of adjunct faculty members (17 of 18 who responded to the question) see achieving coverage as either extremely or very important. Although the number of adjunct faculty members responding to this question is not substantial, it certainly follows that if one's continued employment is dependent upon satisfactorily meeting coverage goals set out by one's employer (the department), achieving those goals would be a top priority.

It is not surprising, then, that for 13 of the 18 adjunct faculty members, lecturing was the chief means of achieving coverage. As the extensive study described by Carol Rutz *et. al.* in "Faculty Professional Development and Student Learning: What is the Relationship?" demonstrates, adjunct faculty members may participate in faculty development opportunities at an even higher rate than tenured faculty members; however, they are far less likely to try new pedagogical approaches in the classroom based on what they have learned because of fear that student ratings will go down (44). Because this study reveals that "More faculty development focused directly on improving teaching and learning directly results in higher performances from students," the significance of faculty status becomes clear: "faculty status matters, not so much because of qualifications but because of job security," with students performing worse in courses taught by faculty members who do not feel free to experiment (44). It is not surprising, then, that the following survey comment critiquing the sense of control lecturing provides was made by a securely tenured faculty member at my university:

> Lecturing, being the sage-on-the-stage imparting knowledge to students, is the most ineffective teaching method for coverage; and yet teachers persist because it gives them a sense of control over the material. Letting students be different in how they approach coverage, through more experiential learning (writing, discussion, peer collaboration), is not as controllable, but it gives students ownership of learning.

What we take from this complex web of influential factors and constraints bearing down on faculty members' ability to cover course material and their choice of what to cover is, again, the importance of teasing out the *reasons* that coverage presents a problem for individual faculty members. While an adjunct in art history and a full professor of physics will share some similar outlooks—based on the survey (not to mention my years of experience as a WAC director), both are primarily concerned with student learning—their perspectives on the importance of coverage and various influences and constraints on how they achieve it will likely be quite different.

In our attempts to open up our colleagues to the potential of writing as a means of coverage, how we respond as WAC directors will depend on the nature of the perceived influences and constraints. Of course, we cannot expect faculty members not to take into account the expectations of accrediting bodies. And given their tenuous status, it would be foolish for contingent faculty members not to honor the course objectives of the departments hiring them. Whereas most faculty members feel a great deal of autonomy over what they do and do not cover (and how), we must honor the realities of those who do not. However, when department policies lead to faculty members feeling unable to work in writing because of the need to cover required material, this might occasion a conversation with the department as a whole (or a sub-set) about learning goals and how they may be achieved. At the very least, the process of reflecting on and discussing constraints to coverage of course material may help faculty members to be more strategic in their thinking about coverage as a course goal. These conversations may illuminate for us the pressure-points about which we might have broader conversations with academic units, ultimately leading to larger-scale change in perspective about coverage. After all, it is only when systemic change takes hold that contingent faculty members will feel freer to diversify pedagogically. Valuing pedagogical experimentation as much as student ratings when evaluating adjunct faculty members—and convincing faculty members that this value is real—is a necessary precursor to their adopting the pedagogical changes that Rutz *et. al.* show lead to higher student performance.

Insight #3: While lecture is the primary means faculty members identify for achieving coverage of course material in their teaching, a majority of faculty members do report changing their means of achieving coverage over time and WAC may have an impact on that.

When asked to rank five means of achieving coverage from most-frequently to least-frequently employed, faculty members ranked them as follows:

1. Lecture
2. Reading
3. Discussion
4. Writing
5. Online

There was some variation among respondent sub-groups, though lecture always holds the #1 spot, even if it is shared with another means of coverage. For example, for WAC faculty members, lecture and reading are listed in equal numbers as the chief means of achieving coverage. Discussion and reading share the #2 spot, writing and reading share the #3 spot, writing is fourth, and online means of content delivery is fifth. For the WAC faculty, then, the importance of writing as a means of achieving coverage is only slightly higher than it is for the faculty respondents as a whole.

However, some faculty members—as illustrated earlier in the comment about how "being the sage-on-the-stage" offers a sense of control—critique lecture as a means of coverage.

> If students do not understand what is "covered" in lecture, it doesn't matter whether it was covered.

> I lecture a little less than I used to—it turns out I'm not so fascinating that I need to be the only one talking for an hour at a time.

While faculty members who had completed the WAC seminar did not rank writing as a means of coverage much more highly than the faculty as a whole, they were most likely to say their methods of achieving coverage had changed over time. Overall, 72 faculty members (77%) report that their methods of achieving coverage have changed over time while 22 (23%) report that they have not. Those most likely to report that their methods have changed include tenure track faculty members and WAC faculty members (both with 86% "yes") and faculty members with 20–30-plus years of teaching experience (83%). Those most likely to report that their means of achieving coverage have not changed are, first, faculty members who have not participated in the WAC seminar (35%) and second, faculty members with 1–6 years of teaching experience (29%).

While it makes sense that faculty members who have been teaching for many years have had more opportunities to change their methods of achieving coverage than those at the start of their teaching careers, it is interesting that whether faculty members have participated in the WAC seminar is the main quality distinguishing those who have changed their strategies for achieving coverage. Of course, it also may be true that faculty members who choose to participate in the WAC seminar are naturally more open to new pedagogies and that participation in the seminar itself did not create this effect. Either way, we do know one thing: WAC faculty members are far more likely to favor "pedagogical diversification" in achieving coverage than non-WAC faculty members and this is something we as WAC directors may leverage, encouraging faculty members to share the various means they use to achieve coverage among themselves and with other faculty members.

Also, as the survey confirmed, faculty members cannot cover material alone. The expectations of students play a significant part in the faculty's ability to achieve coverage of course material. WAC already encourages faculty members to put learning goals first, communicating them clearly to students and scaffolding assignments to support them. We can encourage faculty members to use the language of coverage as they lay out learning goals, communicating clearly with their students about what they expect to cover in a course (and why) and what methods they will use to achieve that coverage. Thus, as the culture of writing spreads across campus, students will repeatedly hear from faculty members that they are going to cover material not only through lecture but also by having students *do* things (including writing). If students hear this more, they too may gain a broader view of coverage, leading to less resistance.

Finally, despite high participation in faculty development, including the WAC seminar at my university, adjunct faculty members feel far less control than tenured faculty members over what course content they cover and how they cover it. Given the increasing numbers of courses taught by adjunct faculty members and given the clear connection between experimentation in teaching and high student performance, addressing issues of coverage beyond the individual faculty-member level is essential if we truly aim to change our institutions' pedagogical cultures. Initiating departmental discussions about what is covered, why, and how may lead to a loosening of both explicitly stated and implicitly assumed constrictions on pedagogical experimentation. The results of these discussions—to which adjuncts, ideally, actively contribute—may free contingent faculty members to act on what they have learned through WAC and other faculty development offerings. I have generated a list of questions to guide such discussions (Appendix).

The next step in this project, for me, will be to begin a series of personal interviews with faculty members who have successfully used writing as a means of achieving coverage, including faculty members across varying disciplines, ranks, and status levels. I will look deeply into their histories with coverage of course content, asking questions such as the following:

- Before they used writing as a means of coverage, what were their learning goals in a typical course and how did they "cover" those goals?
- What influenced their choosing this means of coverage? For example, if they primarily lectured, was it because they had been taught to teach that way? Or had they, as students, learned that way?
- What specifically motivated them to turn to writing as a means of coverage? E.g., did they feel other methods were not working? If so, how did they know? If they completed the WAC seminar, were there elements that were particularly persuasive? Had the change in perspective been coming on for a period of time or was it more of a sudden revelation? What obstacles, both internal and external, did they face?
- How exactly do they use writing assignments to cover course material? How do they know if they have succeeded or not? How are they defining success?

As one faculty member expressed, "Time, time, and time! . . . I feel as if I am running a Marathon!" My survey revealed how emotionally charged the topic of coverage can be for many faculty members. I hope that presenting the stories of colleagues who have struggled with coverage and then developed successful ways of using writing as one means of achieving it will serve as a pressure valve of sorts: naming and providing new perspectives and strategies to address a ubiquitous, but not often discussed, problem. In the end, raising and unpacking ideas about coverage with our faculty colleagues may become a crucial step in achieving the ultimate goal of WAC: to instill and maintain cultures of writing at our colleges and universities.

Notes

1. Other scholars have built upon Calder's "uncoverage" model for history pedagogy. See Hall and Scott, Vickery, and Taillon.

2. In order to be qualified to teach WAC courses at the university (it is a four-course core requirement), faculty members complete a five-day seminar. The seminar addresses the following questions: What does it mean to approach writing as a process as well as a product? What is the relationship of writing to thinking? How can writing be used as a tool for learning subject matter and for critical thinking? What are effective ways to plan, present, sequence, and assess both formal and informal writing assignments? What are helpful and efficient ways to respond to student writing?

3. Approximately 50% (depending on school or college) of faculty evaluation of teaching at my university is based upon student ratings from IDEA surveys. IDEA provides twelve learning objectives and faculty members are evaluated based on the objectives they choose as "essential" or "important" for each course. These objectives range from traditionally coverage-oriented goals such as Objective #1: "Gaining Factual Knowledge (terminology, classifications, methods, trends)" and Objective #2: "Learning fundamental principles, generalizations, and theories" to goals regarding skill acquisition, application of knowledge, and development of dispositions.

Interestingly, faculty members across the disciplines choose objectives 1 and 2—the most content coverage-oriented goals—most frequently. According to an IDEA report ("Disciplinary Selection of Learning Objectives"), for 20 of 28 diverse academic disciplines, the percentage of classes for which instructors selected objectives 1 and/or 2 as essential or important was higher than for any other objective and/or over 80%. Therefore, since faculty members choose these goals, it makes sense that they are concerned about student perceptions of coverage in their courses.

Works Cited

Calder, Lendol. "Uncoverage: Toward a Signature Pedagogy for the History Survey." *The Journal of American History* 92.4. (2006): 1358–70. Print.

Dewey, John. *Experience and Education.* New York: Collier, 1938. Print.

"Disciplinary Selection of Learning Objectives." IDEA website. August 2008. Web. January 2014. <http://ideaedu.org/wp-content/uploads/2014/11/DisciplinaryLearningObjectives.pdf>.

Hall, Timothy D. and Renay Scott. "Closing the Gap Between Professors and Teachers: 'Uncoverage' as a Model of Professional Development for History Teachers." *The History Teacher* 40.2 (2007): 257–63. Print.

Henry, George H. "The Idea of Coverage in the Teaching of Literature." *The English Journal* 54.6.(1965): 475–82. Print.

Reid, E. Shelley. "Uncoverage in Composition Pedagogy." *Composition Studies* 32.1 (2004): 15–34. Print.

Rutz, Carol, et. al. "Faculty Professional Development and Student Learning: What is the Relationship?" *Change: The Magazine of Higher Learning* 44.3 (2012): 40–47. Print.

Taillon, Paul. "'Coverage' and 'Uncoverage': Teaching the U.S. History Survey in New Zealand in Twelve Weeks." *Australian Journal of American Studies* 28.1 (2009): 124–34. Print.

Vickery, Peter. "Progressive Pedagogy in the U. S. History Survey." *Radical Teacher* 83 (2008): 10–13. Print.

Wiggins, Grant, and Jay McTighe. *Understanding by Design.* 2nd ed. Alexandria, VA: ASCD, 2006. Print.

Appendix: A Guide for Departmental Discussions Regarding Coverage of Course Content

1. As a department, what are your common learning goals for this course or set of courses? Are these goals explicitly stated?

2. Where do these goals come from? Departmental consensus and/or outside entities (accreditation or licensure requirements)?

3. What are the primary ways faculty members currently "cover" these goals? (In-class lecture, online lecture, reading, writing, class discussion, other).

4. Regarding *how* faculty members cover the learning goals, how much is your pedagogical choice and how much is determined by implicit or explicit departmental norms? If the latter, how are those norms communicated to faculty members (including adjuncts)?

5. Would the department be open to learning about ways to diversify how learning goals are met?

An Affordance Approach to WAC Development and Sustainability

SHERRY LEE LINKON AND MATTHEW PAVESICH

How can we create institutional change? That remains one of the central puzzles for writing program administrators, especially for those working on writing across the curriculum and/or writing in the disciplines. Dozens of articles and books have addressed this question, arguing for the importance of building relationships, thinking systemically, shifting discursive frames, and more.[1] We want to suggest a different, though related concept: affordances. Psychologist James J. Gibson introduced the term to describe a relation between an object or environment and an organism. The concept has been taken up by many disciplines, including architecture, computer programming, organizational behavior, and more. Within writing studies, affordance has been used most often to articulate the pedagogical and communicative potentials of new media technologies, but we find it equally useful to highlight the way we, as WPAs, both respond to and act on the conditions of our institutional environment.

While affordances sometimes refer to pre-existing and mostly stable physical attributes in organizational and institutional settings, affordances evolve over time, through our responses to and uses of them. In other words, they at once influence what we can do in the local environment and emerge from the actions we take. Our experiences at Georgetown University demonstrate the value of affordance as a way of understanding institutional change and the role of WPAs. In part because it has been used in so many settings, affordance can be a slippery concept, and to make it more concrete, we describe the conditions and development of affordances using the analogy of gardening. We began by tilling fertile soil, prepared over many years by our predecessors but also left fallow in the decade or so before we arrived. Over time, we have added a bit of fertilizer, planted seeds, fertilized a bit more, and spent a lot of time watching things grow. We've also prepared for more growth, building new beds, if you will. Even as we must work with existing conditions, our work is changing the local landscape in ways that establish affordances for the future. At the same time, building any writing program is, like gardening, a cyclical activity that doesn't end with harvesting one season's juicy ripe tomatoes.

Based on our experience at Georgetown, we argue that WAC/WID developers should recognize how our work is at once shaped by and contributes to local affordances. That WPAs must be responsive to local conditions is not news, of course. As Martha Townsend has noted, it is already "axiomatic" that "each institution must grow the program that works within its own constraints and possibilities" (547). The concept of affordances, however, offers three key extensions to this idea. First, if we recognize how our work is both enabled and limited by existing affordances, we can make strategic use of local conditions rather than simply viewing them as obstacles or problems to overcome. Second, if we understand that affordances reflect local history and culture but are also evolving, we can understand our own agency more clearly. Finally, if we see ourselves as developing affordances, we can focus on creating conditions that enable our colleagues' work with writing, rather than on controlling or constraining their work, and this will generate more productive, sustainable outcomes—for our programs and ourselves.

The Uses of Affordances

While a conceptual history of affordance is beyond this article's scope, its migration from psychology into other fields helps frame our use of it in writing program administration. Gibson first coined the term in "The Theory of Affordances" in Robert E. Shaw and John Bransford's *Perceiving, Acting, and Knowing* (1977) and developed it in his book *The Ecological Approach to Visual Perception* (1979). Gibson uses "affordance" to refer to a specific relation between an animal and the material environment. A particular aspect of a physical environment "affords" an animal specific opportunities for action (*Ecological Approach* 127–143). Door-opening devices provide the most common illustrations of affordances: knobs afford twisting and pushing or pulling; plates afford pushing; handles afford pulling. This example suggests why the term found real footing in material design-related fields even though it emerged from psychology. Furthermore, scholars in business and organizational behavior have wedded affordance to habitus in order to consider larger scale practices relative to structure and setting (Weeks and Fayard). Educational researchers use affordance to design curriculum and cultural inclusivity (Barab and Roth; Rasi, Hautakangas, and Vayrynen). User/interface designers and engineers have developed what they call "affordance structure matrices" that map system level affordances to individual components, as in the design of a drilling rig.[2] Some cognitive roboticists consider the ways code can include internal libraries of affordances, recognize affordances, and interact with them (Touretsky and Tira-Thompson). Because it so effectively articulates the relationship between conditions and responses, the concept of affordances has been widely used and adapted.

Gunther Kress is often credited with adapting affordance for writing studies, linking the term to "modes" in a series of arguments on alphabetic text, image, and other interfaces. In Cynthia Selfe and Gail Hawisher's special issue of *Computers and Composition*, "The Influence of Gunther Kress' Work" (2005), published in the wake of his session at the 2004 Conference on College Composition and Communication, some of our leading scholars on multimodality consider Kress's theoretical formulations and impact (Paul Prior, Marilyn Cooper, and Anne Frances Wysocki among them). At bottom, the connection between mode and affordance is relatively simple. Different modes (like the features of material environments) carry different affordances: a handwritten letter allows for stylized script flourishes and sketching with circulatory potential limited to the paper on which it is written, while Facebook limits the font in which one may write but affords the inclusion of other media like photographs and video, as well as wider circulation. Ten years later, affordance and modality in general have so saturated our field that they appear in reference guides like Routledge's *Handbook for Literacy Studies* and Oxford's *A Dictionary of Media and Communication*. They even appear in texts without definition at all.

As in psychology and business, affordance in writing studies has traveled and expanded. Scholars in our field consider affordance at the structural level, as we design interventions into pre-existing environments to bring about desired outcomes. Thinking on this systemic level, we suggest an affordance approach to writing program administration: culture-building through a distributed strategy involving both policy-making and on-the-ground cultivation. As WPAs, we need both to recognize how our work is shaped by existing affordances and actively craft new affordances. To return to the gardening metaphor, we must recognize the affordances of local soil and select the seeds that will grow best in those conditions. We must also fertilize, construct trellises, irrigate, and so on in order to strengthen those conditions.

Existing Affordances: Finding Fertile Soil

Our experiences at Georgetown demonstrate why we find the concept of affordances useful. Long before we could begin acting *on* the local environment, we had to act *in* it, and from the beginning our work was shaped by existing affordances. In 2011, during Matt's first year and just before Sherry was hired, Georgetown completed a self-study for Middle States accreditation that included a proposal to shift students' second encounter with writing from a general education humanities course into the major. As new faculty, we were charged with turning that concept into a proposal, a task that occupied much of our attention during the fall of 2012. After a good deal of reading, a consultation with Terry Myers Zawacki, and attending IWAC 2014—all incredibly valuable experiences for WPAs whose backgrounds lie in scholarship of teaching and learning (Sherry) and rhetoric (Matt)—we crafted a proposal. We had been warned that making change at Georgetown was almost impossible. This is a cautious institution in some ways, and faculty are especially resistant to top-down efforts to change their practices or control their work. Nonetheless, the new "integrated writing" requirement was approved in February, 2013, the first formal change to the institution's core curriculum in thirty years. While colleagues congratulated us on this achievement, we knew that the success of this proposal was rooted in years of prior work. We didn't yet understand just how fertile the soil was, however.

We sensed this fertility early in the process, as we began to meet with department chairs and directors of undergraduate studies (DUS) before drafting the proposal. Many seemed wary of integrating writing into their major, expressing concern about what we might force them to do and explaining why they could not teach writing. Their worries will be familiar to WAC/WID leaders everywhere: writing would distract from content; faculty don't know how to teach grammar; their classes were too large; our oversight would be intrusive. Some insisted that Georgetown's elite students didn't need help with writing, while others claimed that students really needed a basic grammar course—taught by the writing program, of course. We were prepared for these responses, and we tried to assure our colleagues that we understood their concerns and had no desire to become the "writing police."

Yet we also discovered something we hadn't expected: colleagues from several fields responded to our questions with thoughtful and articulate explanations of their disciplines' genres and conventions. The DUS of computer science explained how his students needed to learn to translate their work as designers of software programs and other technologies into language that their clients and funders would understand. The chair of the mathematics and statistics department spoke eloquently about how students needed to master the writing conventions involved in mathematical proofs. It wasn't until we met with the chair of the sociology department that we began to understand what was going on. Offhandedly, he referred to workshops and discussions about the teaching of writing that he'd been part of back in the '80s, when Jim Slevin ran the writing program.

While we had both heard colleagues speak with some reverence of Slevin, who founded the Georgetown writing program in the early 80s, we only recently learned the whole story of the work he and others did to engage faculty in thinking about and teaching writing in the disciplines. As Slevin, Keith Fort, and Patricia E. O'Connor explain in a 1989 report, Georgetown's WID program was always "envisioned and shaped entirely by Georgetown faculty," rather than as a top-down administrative initiative. NEH funds supported annual faculty symposia and workshops that reached more than one hundred faculty from twenty-seven departments across campus. Writing faculty also trained graduate teaching assistants from across campus, since they worked directly with students on writing (14). The article indicates that they were able to create a "permanent" program that was, as of 1989, "entirely supported by the University" (13). The program continued into the early '90s, but it dwindled over time as leading faculty became involved in other projects and as funding was redirected. By the time we arrived, both the active work and the funding had disappeared.

Georgetown had not abandoned attention to teaching, however, nor to writing. In 2000, the university created the Center for New Designs in Learning and Scholarship (CNDLS), directed by Randy Bass, which offers an annual spring teaching conference that regularly includes workshops on the teaching of writing. It also runs a teaching apprenticeship program for graduate students that includes workshops on designing writing assignments and responding to students' writing. CNDLS also sponsored a Teagle Foundation grant for another iteration of work with faculty from across the disciplines, the Georgetown Student Writing Study, led by Maggie Debelius, who was the director of the writing center (she is now director of faculty initiatives at CNDLS). That project, which ran from 2010 to 2012, provided funding and facilitation for teams of faculty from nine programs to examine sample student writing from their programs and develop rubrics for writing in specific projects or courses. The project helped Georgetown address the assessment criteria for institutional accreditation, but it also engaged faculty in conversations about the relationship between writing and threshold concepts in their disciplines. While more modest in scope than the earlier WID project, the Georgetown student writing study similarly encouraged faculty to think about student writing and their teaching.

Both of these projects contributed to the local environment in which we would design, propose, and implement the integrated writing requirement. Because of their work, many faculty across campus were thinking about writing long before we introduced the integrated writing requirement, and they had positive experiences working with faculty from the writing program. These efforts also established some core principles and local expectations about writing: that it is not the property or responsibility of the writing program, that all faculty had expertise in writing, and that we could improve writing education by integrating it into existing courses. Faculty members' prior positive interactions with the writing program fed the soil we would now till.

These elements of our ecosystem function as affordances. As we drafted the proposal for the new writing requirements, we were guided by models from other WID programs to define fairly open-ended criteria, such as asking departments to identify specific courses, to exclude first-year courses, to ask students to write in multiple genres, and to embed writing in smaller courses so that faculty could provide sufficient feedback to students.[3] We also suggested creating a committee that would review proposals and provide feedback. However, Bass, in his role as chair of the core curriculum committee, suggested fewer guidelines and less oversight, though the rationale for this was not immediately clear. As newcomers to Georgetown, we believed that his aim was expedience; Bass wanted to get the requirement passed, even if it was weak. Now we recognize that a shift away from explicit guidelines and review processes reflected the affordances of earlier labor. Both Slevin's faculty-centered, requirement-free approach from the 1980s and Debelius' collaborative, conversational, deductive approach from the more recent past emphasized faculty ownership of writing in their disciplines and an attitude of respect and trust of our colleagues by the writing faculty. Like an architect designing a building to suit a site's affordances, we sought to design a requirement that would not merely respect these existing conditions but would use them strategically. In other words, we needed to design an affordance, not just a requirement.

These affordances allowed us to shape the integrated writing (IW) requirement in a way that Bass termed "legislating the aspiration." Our proposal asked all programs to answer two questions:

- What kinds of writing should our students learn to do?
- How will we help students develop the ability to write effectively in the genres and forms that matter in our field?

Programs had complete control over these strategies; no individual or committee would review or approve them. They could develop any strategy that satisfied them. We asked every program to post its strategy on its website and in the academic bulletin, and we have links to the strategies on the writing program website.[4] This allowed the writing program to position itself as a resource to help colleagues design and implement their strategies, rather than defining us as either the sole experts in writing or the arbiters of sufficient strategies.

While it may appear that by taking an affordance approach we relinquished not only oversight but even the access needed for assessment, we instead have adopted the role Barbara Walvoord calls "the changer": those who "[focus] on faculty change and WAC's impact on change, without trying to define what kind of change it should be" (529). In the two years between the passage of the requirement and the deadline for developing IW strategies, core writing faculty met individually with colleagues from a number of departments and attended some department, college, and committee meetings. We also hosted two working groups, both under the aegis of CNDLS. The first involved teams from four departments that seemed especially well-prepared to address the IW requirement. We consulted separately with each team, but the teams also met together, comparing notes and critiquing each other's approaches. The second cohort focused on individual faculty who wanted to work on teaching writing in their specific courses. We continue to consult with faculty across campus as they develop assignments and teaching strategies in response to the IW requirement and as some programs begin to assess writing in their majors.

More than forty programs have now posted IW strategies, taking varied approaches. A number of programs, especially those in the humanities, identify writing as embedded across the major, from introductory courses through senior capstones. In a typical example, the classical studies major describes the writing students perform at each level of the program:

> ... students at the 100-level write more frequent and shorter papers that develop analytical and argumentative skills. Papers at this level will make use of primary sources (ancient authors, inscriptions, objects) as well as secondary reading (i.e.[,] modern scholarship). At the 200-level, students will write more than they do in 100-level courses, usually in the form of longer assignments that make use of more sources. These courses also typically expect independent student research into specific problems. At the 300 and 400 levels, students write longer research papers which require deep engagement with primary evidence as well as modern scholarship. Students ... progress through a curriculum that develops their writing skills at each step.[5]

Other programs have identified a category of courses in which students write major papers, such as the upper-division seminars in the history and government programs. Some programs require students to take specific courses. Mathematics and statistics identifies three courses that fall near the beginning of the program and address the structure and specialized language of the written proof. Several interdisciplinary programs require all students to write a senior thesis and offer one or two semester courses that provide intensive guidance as students develop these large projects. In the school of nursing and health studies, a first-year seminar is being redesigned around several goals explicitly focused on writing, including writing for reflection and the conventions of writing in the sciences. The biology department created a new sophomore-level course.

The diversity of these approaches reflects the influence of institutional history. On the one hand, that many programs were able to address the requirement by pointing to existing practices suggests a fairly high level of faculty engagement with writing. Of course, some departments dealt with the requirement in this way because they did not want to be bothered. But what WAC or WID program does not have resistant participants? Overall, we have been impressed by our colleagues. A number of programs engaged in department-wide discussions, sometimes with lengthy and contentious debates, and for them the requirement afforded serious consideration of writing in their fields.

Our approach and our colleagues' response to the IW requirement have not only been shaped by the affordances we inherited from our predecessors. Our decisions and our interactions with colleagues, as well our colleagues' work, have also constructed new affordances. To return to the gardening metaphor, we began our round of writing program work with soil that was much more fertile than we initially recognized, and together with colleagues across campus, we've sown our first crops. The question now is how do we continue to use the conditions of the past and those we have helped to create to build a sustainable program? How do we foster a productive campus ecosystem for writing?

Affording Renewable Growth

While Bass described the flexible approach of the integrated writing requirement as "legislating the aspiration," we have come to think it might better be characterized as "constructing an affordance." As the varied programmatic responses suggest, we had designed a flexible requirement that created the conditions for serious conversations about writing within disciplines and programs. Yet without oversight powers, we worried that we might also have legislated ourselves out of position to influence writing instruction on campus. Indeed, we were disappointed that so few of our colleagues responded to our offers of help as they developed IW strategies. We were also concerned that a requirement without standards or review processes would yield little; integrated writing could well turn out to be a requirement in name only. While the results so far are mixed, we believe that the requirement has functioned as an affordance for both our colleagues and the writing program itself. Faculty retained ownership and control, and we have been able to focus on—to return to the gardening metaphor—feeding the soil and collecting seeds that will afford future growth, rather than on weeding. Put differently, the open-ended IW requirement emphasizes our agency rather than potential power. Instead of guarding the gates of writing pedagogy, we have been able to deploy our social and intellectual resources to advance the interests of writing on our campus—as a program, a practice, and a subject of intellectual analysis.

For writing programs, we would argue, deploying this kind of agency is more valuable than securing the power to evaluate or approve our colleagues' work as teachers of writing. If we view our efforts as shaping affordances rather than defending policies, we become not only resources to help colleagues integrate writing pedagogy into their courses but also sources of new opportunities for and ideas about teaching writing. However, as we learned from our experience at Georgetown, we must be attentive to the affordances shaping our work, to opportunities to construct new ones, and to how these affordances enable and/or constrain the work of our colleagues across campus. While our local ecosystem features unique conditions, our attention to affordances offers a strategy that can benefit other WPAs.

As our discussion of the development process suggests, our affordance approach echoes a foundational element of WAC work: coordinating with faculty across the disciplines. As an affordance, our open-ended model invited active engagement by users, and it enabled a diverse range of responses, reflecting particular cases of "filtering" and generating "changes in the user's expectations" in the process (Kannengiesser and Gero 61). To further illustrate the value of viewing WAC/WID efforts as affordances, we offer two additional examples, drawn from the work we have done in the two years since the IW requirement was approved. In each case, our work has been enabled and shaped by affordances that were already in place, and we have, as Udo Kannengiesser and John S. Gero suggest, "interact[ed] with and reason[ed] about" (51) these affordances, generating new affordances in the process.

In the past two years, a major campus innovation project has provided a second affordance that is shaping our work and helping us develop new affordances for both the writing program and our colleagues. "Designing the Future(s) of the University" challenges faculty, staff, and students at Georgetown to imagine new ways of approaching higher education, posing big questions about the structures and processes of liberal arts education.[6] Along with an undergraduate course in which students design the university of the future and a series of presentations about the challenges and opportunities facing higher education in the twenty-first century, "Designing the Future(s)" has supported several faculty-driven, collaborative design projects that are generating new courses, programs, and models. We have been active in several of these projects, positioning the writing program as collaborative and innovative while also heeding Walvoord's admonition that WPA's must either "dive in or die" (70). Most notably, we have been working with colleagues trained in computer science and communication to develop a studio-based undergraduate certificate in writing, design, and communication (CWDC). The CWDC has been designed from the beginning as an experiment to test whether and how a studio-based approach will work—for students, for faculty, and within the structures and practices of the institution.

As an affordance, the CWDC provides two important possibilities for the writing program. First, it has expanded our own thinking about both how we teach writing and the role of the writing program on campus. While some elements of the studio model fit well with common writing pedagogy, such as its attention to process, peer critique, and audience, it also pushes the boundaries of these practices. For example, the certificate replaces coursework with studio time, so that individual and collaborative projects and critiques from faculty, peers, and outside experts provide the primary basis for learning. It also broadens the range of possible student projects to include digital and material artifacts. Both the process of designing the certificate and the experimental framework within which we are working are changing our expectations and encouraging us to rethink our own goals and concepts—even as this process and framework change others' expectations for us and the scope of the writing program.

Additionally, our participation in the CWDC and other "Designing the Future(s)" projects constructs a new affordance for our colleagues across campus by defining the work of teaching writing as flexible, creative, and exploratory and by identifying writing faculty not as representatives of a body of already-established theories and practices but as scholars engaged in innovation and collaboration. These efforts are in their early stages, but responses so far suggest that, if nothing else, they are broadening our colleagues' sense of who we are, what we do, and what writing can be.

Our interest in creating affordances for our colleagues dovetails with one final example, our approach to assessment. Georgetown has lagged behind national trends in assessment, and many faculty resist what they see as an externally-imposed and largely meaningless, unrewarded, and time-consuming activity. However, the 2012 Middle States accreditation review explicitly asked the university to develop its assessment of writing, and by 2017, we must report to the accrediting agency on our assessment efforts. In 2013, we began a standard assessment practice, collecting sample papers from our first-year writing course and reviewing them using a rubric based on the course goals, with the idea that we would define a benchmark against which we could measure improvement in the program.[7] Given the range of assignments and strategies used in our first-year writing course, this model proved problematic, as it so often does, and the results were uninspiring and predictable. Meanwhile, the open-ended design of the integrated writing requirement and our efforts to avoid being defined as "the writing police" made us wary of evaluating the work of other departments or their students, and faculty resistance to assessment made it clear that we could not demand that programs conduct their own assessments of students' writing. We needed a better approach. At the same time, we were beginning to articulate the idea that our work was creating affordances for our colleagues, and we wanted to test that idea and seek out further opportunities for helping to shape a "culture of writing" at Georgetown.

All of this led us to institutional ethnography (IE) (LaFrance and Nicholas). A presentation from University of Michigan faculty at the 2014 International Writing Across the Curriculum Conference (Gere, Silver, and Pugh) and subsequent consultation with Michelle LaFrance helped us recognize the affordances of this approach. IE treats the object of study, in this instance the work of our writing program and the effects of that work distributed across the university, as a complex system. As Julie Jung suggests, "a complex system cannot be understood by reducing it to its component parts, since it's the *interaction* among parts and not the sum of their individual properties that produces macrolevel behaviors attributable to the system as a whole" (11). We hoped that institutional ethnography would allow us to trace interactions and understand how they were shaping writing in the campus ecosystem. We have already begun studying samples of student writing and course syllabi, surveying students and faculty, and conducting focus groups that build on survey results. Like other aspects of our work, IE positions us not as judges but as scholars and explorers, roles that are valued on a research-oriented campus. IE works within but also examines local structural, social, economic, and political conditions. It considers how faculty work structures—the nature of labor contracts but also the organization and functioning of four very different undergraduate schools and dozens of majors—affect how we teach writing. It also engages faculty and students across campus in the process and defines assessment not as an act of judgment but as an opportunity for us to learn. So far, colleagues have responded enthusiastically to invitations to focus groups and interviews. Those who are anxious about the writing program intruding on academic freedom or judging their work are less likely to feel threatened by an ethnographic project, which emphasizes exploring the culture of writing rather than on evaluating students' writing and, by implication, faculty instruction.

Even more important, we believe, the ethnography will, like our initial round of conversations, generate insights that will help us understand and respond productively to existing affordances in ways that will foster engagement with and excitement about writing at Georgetown. We have framed the ethnography around two core questions:

- What variables—faculty status and perspectives, disciplinary expectations, institutional resources, curriculum and pedagogical design, student experience, and so on—shape people's teaching and learning about writing?
- What opportunities for strengthening the culture of writing at Georgetown emerge from this analysis?

By pursuing these questions, we hope to develop a descriptive analysis that we can share with our colleagues as another means of defining both our role and ways of thinking about writing. It will also suggest opportunities for further work for the writing program. In other words, our ethnography will generate new affordances, for us and for our colleagues.

Conclusion

Our circumstances at Georgetown are unique. Of course they are. We're not advocating that colleagues do what we did. Everyone's circumstances demand specific responses. We're advocating a disposition, a perspective and pose that we bring to WAC/WID development and writing program administration more generally. Viewing our work as responding to and developing affordances allows us to productively address one of the long-term challenges that most WAC/WID programs face: sustainability. In a 2012 chapter about program "vulnerability," Martha Townsend discusses the "devolutions" of some WAC programs, and she lists the "characteristics of successful WAC programs," including faculty ownership, administrative support, and mission symbiosis. We're struck, however, by characteristic 15: "patience and vigilance" (554). She quotes David Russell, noting that WAC requires, "personal sacrifices . . . and offers personal rather than institutional rewards" (554). While this may be true for many, because an affordance approach requires flexibility and responsiveness from both the writing program and faculty in other disciplines, we believe that it can help us develop sustainable WAC programs that need not rely so heavily on the patience and vigilance of WPAs.

This focus on change shifts our attention away from the completion of a product—a WAC/WID program centered on a well-defined set of rules and practices that we must then defend—toward attention to ongoing coordination. It defines us as agents of change who respond actively to fluid conditions and emerging opportunities. Rather than establishing and preserving our power to define what "counts" as good enough writing instruction, we can enable and facilitate our colleagues' work with student writing and respond to their unpredictable reformulations. This approach also assigns to our colleagues the responsibility for attention to writing, a move that respects their expertise even as it calls upon them to do their own thinking about what their students need and how their programs will work. No doubt, being responsive takes time and energy, but it also allows us to be adaptive and thus more effective.

An affordance approach also changes how we interact with other people on campus. We're less interested in training individuals and cultivating particular allies than we are in crafting environmental affordances that don't require the perpetual investment of professor X, department chair Y, and associate dean Z. We also hope that these affordances depend less on us as sustainers of integrated writing, that our affordances will allow us to accomplish what Jeff Grabill identifies as the work of rhetoric itself: "to assemble a . . . public around a matter of concern and to care for that assembly" (258). If the aspiration we legislated is Grabill's "matter of concern," our writing program's increasing involvement with innovative initiatives on campus is how we "care for that assembly."

Finally, and perhaps most significantly, viewing our work in terms of affordances encourages us to pursue the intellectual curiosity and programmatic creativity that can keep WPAs engaged and energized as professionals. On a basic but crucial level, we hope that this approach will enable us to find more pleasure and meaning in our work. We will find more value in being creative inventors, researchers, and collaborators, rather than vigilant enforcers. We'll likely never be entirely free from the frustration of resistant colleagues, and we cannot protect our programs from budget cuts or changing institutional priorities more than any other WPAs. But an affordance model does make us and our programs less vulnerable to burnout or institutional problems.

This may provide an answer to the question we posed at the beginning of this essay. How do we create institutional change? We don't. We contribute to the conditions that enable change. The concept of affordances reminds us that the real job of WPAs is to create possibility rather than hierarchy and to remain mindful of the nature of agency. We are always in motion with resources and partners, things and people, and while we never bring any real control to bear, we always and happily work in fluid call and response. To return to the gardening metaphor one last time, even the most assiduous gardener must work in partnership with the soil, the climate, and the seed. And for many, that is where the pleasure lies.

Notes

1. We've been influenced especially by Condon and Rutz; Fulwiler and Young; McLeod, Miraglia, Soven, and Thaiss; McLeod and Soven; and Monroe.

2. http://www.iadc.org/wp-content/uploads/ASM_Concept.pdf.

3. We found Pamela Flash's work on the "Writing-Enhanced Curriculum" at the University of Minnesota and the consultative model used at Quinnipiac University especially helpful, since both focused on facilitating departmental conversations about writing rather than on "training" faculty or establishing formal guidelines.

4. To see the integrated writing strategies, visit our website, writing.georgetown.edu and click on the "For Faculty" tab.

5. http://classics.georgetown.edu/Integrated%20Writing.

6. To learn more about these initiatives, visit the "Designing the Future(s)" project website at https://futures.georgetown.edu/about/.

7. Along with developing the IW requirement, we also revised the first-year writing course and began regular faculty development, so we hoped to see change over time.

Works Cited

Barab, Sasha A., and Wolff-Michael Roth. "Curriculum-Based Ecosystems: Supporting Knowing from an Ecological Perspective." *Educational Researcher* 35.5 (2006): 3–13. Web. 14 May 2015.

Condon, William, and Carol Rutz. "A Taxonomy of Writing Across the Curriculum Programs: Evolving to Serve Broader Agendas." *College Composition and Communication* 64.2 (2012): 357–82. Print.

Fulwiler, Toby, and Art Young, eds. *Programs That Work: Models and Methods for Writing Across the Curriculum*. Portsmouth, NH: Boynton/Cook Publishers, 1990. Print.

Gere, Anne Ruggles, Naomi Silver, and Melody Pugh. "Interrogating Disciplinarity in WAC/WID: An Institutional Ethnography." University of Minnesota. The Commons Hotel, Minneapolis, MN. 13 June 2014. Panel Presentation.

Gibson, James J. "The Theory of Affordances." Shaw, Robert, and John Bransford. *Perceiving, Acting, and Knowing: Toward an Ecological Psychology*. Hillsdale, NJ: Lawrence Erlbaum Associates, 1977. 67–82. Print.

—. *The Ecological Approach to Visual Perception*. Boston: Houghton Mifflin, 1979. Print.

Grabill, Jeff. "The Work of Rhetoric in the Common Places: An Essay on Rhetorical Methodology." *JAC* 34.1–2 (2014): 247–67. Print.

Jung, Julie. "Systems Rhetoric: A Dynamic Coupling of Explanation and Description." *Enculturation* 17 (2014): n. pag. Web. 9 April 2014.

Kannengiesser, Udo, and John S. Gero. "A Process Framework of Affordance Design." *DesignIssues* 28.1 (2012): 50–62. Web. 15 June 2015.

LaFrance, Michelle, and Melissa Nicholas. "Institutional Ethnography as Materialist Framework for Writing Program Research and the Faculty-Staff Work Standpoints Project." *College Composition and Communication* 64.1 (2012): 130–50. Print.

McLeod, Susan H., and Eric Miraglia. "Writing Across the Curriculum in a Time of Change.". McLeod, Miraglia, Soven, and Thaiss 1–27.

McLeod, Susan H., Eric Miraglia, Margot Soven, and Christopher Thaiss, eds. *WAC for the New Millennium: Strategies for Continuing Writing-Across-The-Curriculum Programs*. Urbana, IL: NCTE, 2001. Print.

McLeod, Susan H., and Margot Soven. *Writing Across the Curriculum: A Guide to Developing Programs*. Newbury Park, CA: Sage Publications, 1992. Web. 2 June 2015.

Monroe, Jonathan, ed. *Local Knowledges, Local Practices: Writing in the Disciplines at Cornell*. Pittsburgh: U of Pittsburgh P, 2003. Print.

Rasi, Paivi, Mikko Hautakangas, and Sai Vayrynen. "Designing culturally inclusive affordance networks into the curriculum." *Teaching in Higher Education* 20.2 (2015): 131–42. Web. 15 May 2015.

Selfe, Cynthia, and Gail Hawisher. "The Influence of Gunther Kress' Work." *Computers and Composition: An International Journal for Teachers of Writing* 22.1 (2005): 1–100. Print.

Slevin, James, Keith Fort, and Patricia E. O'Connor. "Georgetown University." *Programs That Work: Models and Methods for Writing Across the Curriculum*. Ed. Toby Fulwiler and Art Young. Portsmouth, NH: Boynton/Cook, 1990. 9–28. Print.

Touretzky, David S., and Ethan Tira-Thompson. "Affordances: Cognitive Robotics." Carnegie-Mellon University. 23 March 2008. Web. 14 May 2015.

Townsend, Martha. "WAC Program Vulnerability and What To Do About It: An Update and Brief Bibliographic Essay." *Writing Across the Curriculum: A Critical Sourcebook*. Ed. Terry Myers Zawacki and Paul M. Rogers. Boston: Bedford/St. Martin's, 2012. 543–56. Print.

Walvoord, Barbara. "The Future of WAC." *College English* (1996): 58–79. Web. 24 August 2015.

Weeks, John, and Anne-Laure Fayard. "The Affordance of Practice—The Influence of Structure and Setting on Practice." *Faculty & Research Working Paper: INSEAD, The Business School for the World* (2007): 1–37. Web. 30 May 2015.

"Emphasizing Similarity" but Not "Eliding Difference": Exploring Sub-Disciplinary Differences as a Way to Teach Genre Flexibly

KATHERINE L. SCHAEFER

Rebecca Nowacek, in her 2009 paper, "Why Is Being Interdisciplinary so Very Hard to Do? Thoughts on the Perils and Promise of Interdisciplinary Pedagogy," suggests that instructors can highlight disciplinary differences in genre expectations as a way to help students understand writing more deeply. In this paper, Nowacek describes her observations of a writing-intensive, team-taught general education course composed of three overlapping course units, each drawing on one of three disciplines: literature, history, or religion. She noted that the three disciplinary instructors thought that they were assigning the same genre, an essay, but had very different views on what an essay should do, or indeed, what it meant to have a thesis. Furthermore, she observed that students noticed this issue, and that instructors, when called upon to respond, tended to focus on "emphasizing similarity, [and] eliding difference" (p. 505). Drawing on cultural-historical-activity theory (Engeström, 1987; Roth & Lee, 2007; Russell, 1995), she analyzes the reasons for the disagreement, and the "double binds" that the students found themselves in when they could not resolve the conflicts. She further explores how the instructors might have responded. In the end, she says:

> Both students and instructors, I argue, must negotiate double binds placed upon them when various disciplines conflict. These double binds can limit and constrain the work of individuals, but if made an object of reflection, the double bind can also facilitate higher-order thinking about disciplines and the role of writing within them. (p. 494)

When I discovered this paper, I responded strongly to the idea of eliding differences. I—once an assistant professor specializing in cellular immunology and now an immunologist working as a "writing in the disciplines" (WID) specialist within a writing program—have, for four years running, co-taught a biology laboratory course with Cheeptip Benyajati, a faculty member in the biology department. We initially planned to co-teach every writing instruction session but emphasized to ourselves and to the students that she would maintain responsibility for biology content questions, while I would focus on attention to writing principles. However, this plan was complicated by my years as a practicing biologist; I frequently found myself speaking with biology insider knowledge in response to student questions, and Tip encouraged this tendency, arguing that it helped model scientific discussion. Furthermore, when I did speak as a biologist, she sometimes disagreed and asked questions—and I found myself almost reflexively trying to claim that we were in agreement. In short, I was "emphasizing similarity" and "eliding differences."

Furthermore, I noticed that we didn't disagree about writing principles or, as Tip said, about "what it means to do good science"; we had similar epistemological orientations. Nor did we disagree about the essentials of the genre we asked them to use: the Introduction-Methods-Result-Discussion (IMRD) research article, or the rhetorical moves (Swales, 1990, 2004) within this structure. Instead, I thought our choices might be traced to subtle differences in rhetorical exigencies and conventions typical of particular sub-disciplinary communities (Thaiss & Zawacki, 2006); although we are both biologists, molecular biologists and cellular immunologists are somewhat different. While there could of course be other reasons than disciplinary specialization for our disagreement, this line of reasoning got me thinking: could our experience, combined with Nowacek's suggestions about creating opportunities for reflections on differences, point at a way of emphasizing genre flexibility and the ways that different disciplinary sub-communities use the genre *within* a scientific discipline?

Put more broadly, might Nowacek's suggestion be applicable even when the instructors are from the same discipline? In the rest of this essay, I will attempt to answer this question, drawing on both published literature and our own experience, and argue that widely disparate disciplines are not necessary to set up conflicts that can be made the object of reflection. Professors *within* a discipline may well have areas of disagreement within a single genre that can be exploited. If made the focus of reflection and discussion, these differences can help faculty members to make explicit their implicit knowledge of communication within their specialty areas (Becher & Trowler, 2001; Berkenkotter & Huckin, 1995b; Duff, 2010; Prior, 1995, 1998; Russell, 1995) and relate communicative choices to disciplinary rhetorical exigencies. In addition, they can help students to understand what it means to be a part of a wide-ranging discipline containing several areas of specialization and subtly different types of writing tasks, as well as to see how disciplines, and the rhetorical situations and choices associated with them, change over time (Bazerman, 1984, 1988; Berkenkotter & Huckin, 1995a; Vande Kopple, 2000). This approach should help students see genres not as static recipes, but as tools that both shape researchers and are shaped by researchers in response to evolving needs (Bazerman, 1988; Berkenkotter & Huckin, 1993; Prior, 1998).

Disciplines, Sub-Disciplines, and Overlapping Activity Systems

While there are many possible definitions of disciplines and sub-disciplines (Thaiss & Zawacki, 2006), I will use Becher & Trowler's (2001) approach, which captures three epistemological attributes. A first involves the fundamental disciplinary questions (MacDonald, 1987). The second is one of disciplinary stance, or whether the members of the discipline want to know how a phenomenon works or envision applying the knowledge to solve a problem (Biglan, 1973). Finally, it is important to consider whether the practitioners espouse a normalized viewpoint, attempting to accumulate knowledge that has been "proven," using agreed-upon theoretical frameworks, or tend toward a more reflexive approach that consistently questions these frameworks (Kuhn, 1977). While this is a reductionist approach that risks reifying fluid situations (Hyland, 2004a), it does provide a useful framework. As such, research disciplines are often classified according to where they fall on the Biglan classification scale (Biglan, 1973), which consists of three axes that roughly correspond, respectively, to these epistemological dimensions: *life/non-life, pure/applied,* and *hard/soft.*

Disciplinary communities can be further divided into sub-disciplines. In the simplest formulation, a sub-discipline is simply an area of specialization originally found within a parent discipline (Thaiss & Zawacki, 2006). However, as a result of specialization, the sub-discipline has adopted a recognizable focus on a particular type of question and/or epistemologies and methodologies and exhibits its own culture (Becher & Trowler, 2001). For the purposes of this paper, I describe (sub-)disciplines largely in terms of their Biglan characteristics. However, I do not mean this definition to be limiting, and suspect that the teaching applications and research questions that my work suggests could be applied within a wide variety of definitions.

Disciplines and sub-disciplines can also roughly map onto the activity systems described by cultural-historical-activity theory, making the connection to Nowacek's (2009) work clearer. In its simplest formulation (Nowacek, 2009; Russell, 1995), an activity system consists of a *subject* (person(s); here, the investigators), the *object* (what they are studying), the *motives* for their activity (their reasons for study), and the *tools* that they use to accomplish the work (disciplinary and discursive). Specializations or sub-disciplines that differ in object, motives, and/or tools from others are working within similar but not identical activity systems. However, while I think it is useful to think of sub-disciplines as overlapping activity systems within a larger disciplinary grouping, I do not mean to entirely equate sub-disciplines and activity systems. Even a disciplinary specialization is a large activity group; within any activity group that roughly shares object, motive, and tools, there are still smaller possible activity groups: investigators at a particular university, in a particular time, or from a particular research group—even down to a partnership between two researchers.

Several cautionary tales (Beaufort, 2007; Nowacek, 2009; Russell & Yañez, 2003) make it clear that students with writing experience in one discipline (activity system) have difficulty transferring that knowledge to another discipline (activity system) when they are asked to write using a particular discursive tool or genre (e.g., a thesis-driven essay, or a book-report) that looks superficially identical to the one from the first discipline. A major source of their difficulty lies in the fact that they do not have sufficient disciplinary knowledge to understand how the superficially similar form normally serves a very different purpose, to look at different objects and/or for different motives. In this paper, I also explore how the same issue might be true when making smaller changes: when moving from one sub-discipline or activity group to another.

Disciplinary and Sub-Disciplinary Choices within the IMRD Structure

Because epistemological considerations have important implications for the way that investigators communicate (Berkenkotter & Huckin, 1995b; Hyland, 2004b; Petraglia, 1995; Russell, 1995; Swales, 1990), it is not surprising that discourse communities (as defined by Bizzell, 1992) that use the Intro-Methods-Results-Discussion (IMRD) genre make recognizably different choices depending on the precise (sub-)discipline. These differential choices occur because the exigencies of a particular type of inquiry lead to recurring rhetorical situations (Miller, 1984) that can be addressed in similar ways (Bazerman, 1988; Berkenkotter & Huckin, 1995b; Prior, 1998; Swales, 1990). These similarities lead to particular types of solutions that include patterns of reasoning that draw on the epistemologies and values of the particular discipline (Toulmin, 1958) and, over time, give rise in turn to genres and choices within the genres that "signal a discourse community's norms, epistemology, ideology, and social ontology" (Berkenkotter & Huckin, 1993, p. 497).

Below, I review two types of signals that have been especially well-characterized with respect to differences between disciplines and sub-disciplines: rhetorical moves and the linguistic mechanisms that authors use to signal stance and engagement. These signals are especially accessible to instructors considering highlighting differences.

Rhetorical Moves

Drawing on multiple previous corpus analyses, Swales (1990) argued that research articles across a great range of disciplines could be characterized in terms of a limited number of canonical rhetorical moves. Initially, this idea was best elaborated with respect to Introductions, using the Create-A-Research-Space (CARS) series of rhetorical moves (p. 141). Move 1 is used in "establishing territory"; move 2 in "establishing a niche"; and move 3 in "occupying a niche." Within the moves, there are further canonical "step" choices; for instance, an author "establishing territory" might do so by "claiming centrality" or "making topic generalizations." Introductions can use simple M1-M2-M3 structure (Swales, 1990), or cycle, as in M1-M2-M1-M3 (Swales, 2004). This initial framework inspired Swales and others to codify a similar series of moves for the methods, results, and discussion sections, as well as to examine variation within those sections. The outcomes of these analyses suggest that both disciplines and sub-disciplines make recognizable choices in all of these areas, in ways that reflect their rhetorical needs.

Swales (1990) summarized broad disciplinary differences in the introductions, noting that the move 1, step 1 option of "establishing centrality" (p. 141) is less common in the hard sciences. The tendency to outline purposes versus principal results, to explain the importance of the findings, or road-map the paper (move 3) also varies by discipline. In addition to these disciplinary differences, several studies suggest recognizable differences in sub-disciplines. Samraj (2002, 2005) found that writers in two sub-disciplines of biology make different step choices within the M1-M2-M3 structure, as do writers in three engineering sub-disciplines (Kanoksilapatham, 2012). Similarly, Ozturk (2007) showed that two applied linguistics sub-disciplines chose different move cycling patterns. In all cases, the authors argued that the stereotypical differences were related to underlying differences in the sub-disciplines' Biglan classifications.

Swales (2004) noted that the biggest disciplinary differences appear in the methods and results sections. Methods sections contain very "clipped" descriptions in hard fields with well-established methodology, but use an "elaborated" version in softer fields with more variation (p. 220). Similarly, in the results sections, writers in disciplines in which the methodologies and interpretational methods are not well-established are more prone to use persuasive moves to justify their choices. And while all writers review their findings and integrate them into the larger field in the discussion section, the amount of self-promotion varies widely by discipline. Kanoksilapatham (2012) also codified rhetorical move and step choices in the methods, results, and discussion sections within three engineering sub-disciplines and found recognizable sub-disciplinary differences in all three sections.

Stance and Engagement

Drawing on a decade of his own work, as well as earlier work by Swales (1990), Hyland (2005) proposed that interactions with the audience can be mediated by two classes of linguistic resources: stance and engagement features. *Stance* refers to the ways in which "writers present themselves and convey their judgments, opinions, and commitments," while *engagement* refers to the ways in which writers "acknowledge and connect to others" (p. 176). Engagement strategies are those that include the reader in some way, and are designed to "meet readers' expectations of inclusion and disciplinary solidarity" or to "rhetorically position the audience" (p. 182). Stance markers include hedges, boosters, attitude markers, and self-mention; engagement markers include reader pronouns, personal asides, appeals to shared knowledge, directives, and questions.

Using this classification scheme, Hyland (2005) examined research articles from eight disciplines, two of which were sub-disciplines of a larger engineering discipline. Hyland found that the hard disciplines had a lower level of both stance and engagement markers than the soft disciplines. Hedges were the most frequently used stance resource in all disciplines, but the soft disciplines used nearly twice as many. Hyland speculated that these differences reflect variation in the degree to which a discipline has agreed-upon ways of making claims; when the criteria for acceptance are less clear, it pays to hedge and also to try to use engagement markers to persuade through "sympathetic understanding, promoting tolerance in readers through an ethical rather than a cognitive progression" (p.187). Notably, electrical engineering and mechanical engineering writing showed differences in both stance and engagement markers, suggesting that even disciplines that are in roughly the same space on the hard/soft and pure/applied axes may have cultures and needs that promote different choices.

A Case Study: A Molecular Biologist Co-Teaches With a Cellular Immunologist

At least within the level of specificity appropriate for writing at the undergraduate level, Tip and I did not have serious disagreements about rhetorical moves or stance and engagement markers (although other co-instructors might well have). However, we encountered other areas of disagreement. After systematically exploring the differences between writing in our sub-disciplines and discussing the reasons for our preferences, we uncovered several possible explanations. I offer this reflection on our experience as a way to explore how instructors might use initially disparate expectations as a starting point for articulating their own reasons for their writing choices.

Background of the Instructors and Course

During our PhD work, both Tip and I were pure molecular biologists; post-PhD, I switched to cellular immunology. These two fields share a common hard epistemology, and have considerable overlap in experimental techniques and some specialist journals. However, they differ in the fundamental problems being studied, some of the methodologies and specialist journals, the funding mechanisms, the speed of the research, and the histories of their fields (Levin, 2006), as well as in their position on the pure/applied scale (my approach to cellular immunology, at least, was well into the applied realm).

Our course served juniors and seniors with a declared biology major, many of whom go on to health-professions or graduate schools. The biology major at our small R1 university encompasses six different specialist tracks (e.g., biochemistry, ecology and evolution, etc.), and this course could be used to partially satisfy the requirement for laboratory research for three of the six tracks. Many, but not all, of the students had prior or concurrent experience doing independent research in some aspect of biology or an allied discipline like epidemiology or chemistry.

This course included writing for both "writing-to-learn" and "learning-to-write" (Russell, 2002, p. 311) purposes. We hoped that by writing, students would explore the underlying scientific concepts more deeply; we also wanted them to learn to communicate the process of science using a widely-accepted genre: the research article. In the instructions for their three research write-ups, we explicitly asked the students to write as if they were writing a scientific research article, and our explanations, while they did not explicitly use Swales' (1990) terminology, heavily reflected his concepts of rhetorical moves within an Intro-Methods-Results-Discussion (IMRD) structure. For instance, while we did not use the words *rhetorical move* we did tell students that, in the introduction, the first paragraph gives background (a.k.a. move 1); the second identifies a question or gap in the literature (move 2); and the third provides a preview of the paper (move 3). We asked for an elaborated methods style; similarly, in the results, we asked students to outline their methodology and interpret their findings, as generally happens in disciplines with sufficient heterogeneity to make this necessary (Swales, 2004).

We offered writing instruction in the form of three genre analysis-based workshops with peer discussion. The first workshop focused on figures and figure legends, as these were the fundamental reporting units from each laboratory session. The second, in preparation for writing the first full laboratory report, involved discussing the reasons for the IMRD structure, as well as identifying key rhetorical moves in one sample paper. The third focused on identifying rhetorical moves within all IMRD sections in multiple papers, and integrating what students discovered with comments that teaching assistants (acting as disciplinary insiders) had made on the student lab reports. All workshops drew on examples from a four-paper sample paper set, picked with several ideas in mind. First, the paper set represented the departmental discourse community; it contained papers from three biology department professors (including Tip) and one from me. In addition, the set contained necessary background knowledge about procedures, materials, and methods. Finally, the papers were meant to serve as general models for the type of report the students were writing, and also contain examples of specialized types of writing tasks (e.g., derivation of equations). All papers were published between 1997 and 2001 (Benyajati et al., 1997; Culver & Noller, 1999; Schaefer & McClure, 1997; Sia, Dominska, Stefanovic, & Petes, 2001).

Example #1: Different Expectations About Figure Legend Titles

Figure legends in scientific research articles convey a great deal of critical information in a small space. Ideally, a disciplinary insider should be able to understand the paper's important information just based on the visual elements in a figure and the associated figure legends, without recourse to the larger text.

Tip (Benyajati, 2012) wrote explicit instructions on how to write the figure legend titles:

> A descriptive title that refers to the general type of experiment done. This should give the reader a good idea of the experiment and the technique, but not the details (e.g.: "Restriction digest analysis of TOP transformants on an agarose gel," NOT "2% agarose gel run at 100V"). (p. 10)

This style has two key elements, as executed in most research papers: (1) focus on the methodology, not the result and (2) a sentence fragment form.

When I saw this instruction, I didn't question it. It seemed reasonable, as I had indeed written (in 1997) figure legend titles in this form and the sample paper set contained one of my papers written with that style. However, I was also aware that alternatives existed; in papers that I published after 1997, I used a different form: one that emphasizes the experimental logic and conclusion of the experiment and is formed as a complete sentence.

The difference is illustrated below, in an excerpt of figure legends taken from a paper that Tip wrote (Benyajati et al., 1997):

> Figure 2: *Western blot analysis* using domain-specific antibodies.

> Figure 3: GAGA-519 and GAGA-581 *factors bind* a single GAGA sequence *forming* multiple-related nucleoprotein *complexes*.

Figure 2 is a clear example of the first methodological type; it focuses on the technique (italicized) and does not contain information about the results of that analysis. In contrast, figure 3 is in conclusion style; while it hints about the method (something about binding and complexes), it primarily states a conclusion, expressed as a complete sentence: factors bind, forming complexes.

While I didn't question the instructions, I did notice that I tended to have off-the-cuff answers to student questions that took the conclusion style; I would almost always answer in a complete sentence, as in "Western blot analysis shows protein expression." But rather than explore this issue, I simply corrected myself and moved on, even though the excerpt above suggests that there might be considerable variation in this choice, even within a single paper. What was going on? I initially assumed that this was a sub-disciplinary matter, because I had used the experimental focus form exclusively in my two papers that I had written as a molecular biologist; a scant two years later, as an immunologist, six of my eight figure legends were in conclusion style. My idea was further supported by an analysis of the sample paper set—all from molecular biologists—that we gave the students to analyze. In those four papers, with twenty experimental figure legends, only two were of the conclusion style, and three of the four papers in the set had no conclusion-style legends.

However, while my hunch was not unreasonable, I could imagine other possible factors, including publication date, the author's home country, the difficulty of encapsulating the whole take-home message, the ease with which the author thinks the audience can identify the take-home message, the sub-disciplinary experimental logic, and individual stylistic preference. To my knowledge, a corpus analysis of figure legend choices has not yet been done in any discipline, so it was hard to say if disciplines or sub-disciplines make recognizably different choices in these areas. Thus, I did a rudimentary analysis of these two extremes in figure legend title formats. (It is not my intention here to do a formal corpus analysis but simply to reflect on a major source of variation that I was able to easily pick out.)

I analyzed figure legend titles from *Nucleic Acids Research (NAR)* and from the *Journal of Immunology (JI)*. Both journals are well-regarded specialist journals for, respectively, the molecular biology and immunology communities. In order to examine trends over time, I month-and-year-matched both my and Tip's sample paper set papers in both journals, as well as examining the most recent issue. I then collated all of the figure legends, excluding purely schematic (data-free) figures, and identified those with titles in the conclusion-style complete sentence format, asking a scientist colleague to randomly spot-check five percent of my assignments (we scored the same way one hundred percent of the time). The results are shown in Table I:

This analysis suggested that my hunch was correct: there are sub-disciplinary differences in the tendency to express the figure legend title as a complete, conclusion-style sentence. However, it also appears that this tendency has been increasing over time in both communities and that there can be significant variation even within a paper. While there are sub-disciplinary factors affecting the choice, there are clearly additional ones.

Table I: Both publication year and journal affect likelihood of expressing the figure legend as a complete sentence.

Journal	Year	Volume (Issue)	No. Papers	No. Legends	% C form legends	% papers with 100% C style
Nucleic Acids Research	1997	25(16)	28	114	5.3	7.1
	1999	27(3)	28	120	10.8	3.6
	2015	43(10)	34	195	47.2	26.5
Journal of Immunology	1997	159(3)	60	381	19.2	5.0
	1999	162(3)	80	475	27.6	5.0
	2015	194(11)	49	319	63.0	38.8

All data-driven articles (excluding commentary, summary, and reviews) appearing within the print volume were analyzed; figure (but not table) legends were included if they contained data (schematic figures excluded). *C style* refers to a conclusion style, with subject and verb.

When I showed Tip this analysis, she noted that she had expected the trend toward conclusion-style legends in both sub-disciplines. Her explanation—one that I agree with—was that this preference reflects the increasing speed of scientific research in all biology sub-disciplines. When readers have to get through a lot, it speeds processing if the author states the result right up front. Similarly, the rapid growth of research techniques, even within a specialty area, necessitates helping the readership draw conclusions, as the author can't be sure that the reader is familiar with any particular technique. She also noted that competition for funding has increased over time, making it more desirable to describe each finding as an exciting conclusion. To explain the fact that, despite the overall increase, *NAR* writers still use fewer conclusion-style legend titles than *JI* writers, she suggested that the *NAR* community has a more constrained set of techniques, and possibly less competitive funding sources, perhaps reducing the need for clearly stated (and exciting) conclusions.

Tip's analysis is highly congruent with Berkenkotter and Huckin's (1995a) analysis of how physicists and biologists read and write IMRD research articles: as a search for "news value" (p. 28). They found that experienced scientists reading in their specialty area first scanned for important new information, by reading the title, abstract, and results sections (including figures and tables). They further argue, based on an analysis of the evolution of elements within the IMRD structure over time, that writers—under pressure from an ever-increasing volume of scientific knowledge as well as real promotional needs related to funding—have made changes to the form that help readers perform this scanning function and see the information as newsworthy. These changes include more informative titles, addition and then expansion of the abstract, sub-headers, and a statement of results at the end of the introduction.

While their analysis did not extend to figure legend titles, the increasing trend toward providing a complete sentence mini-summary in the figure legend title can easily be seen as part of the adaptation to pressures for newsworthiness (one that seems to have gained speed after 1995).

It is clear that our difference of opinion—and, as is clear after our discussions, the disparity between our instructions and the way we ourselves read and write research articles—were interesting from a rhetorical point of view, and we were probably doing the students a disservice by not exploring the difference. Not only were students seeing this sort of variation in one of the papers that we provided as a model, but they were additionally almost certainly seeing similar variation in papers they were reading for other classes or their independent research projects. Our choice, both to codify and to fail to follow up on a difference in choices that I was clearly finding difficult to suppress, may well have confused the students (although I don't have that information). In addition, we had in effect treated genres as static, rather than fluid (Ramanathan & Kaplan, 2000; Smit, 2004) and missed an opportunity to discuss how the field and affiliated writing choices had changed over time (Bazerman, 1984, 1988; Berkenkotter & Huckin, 1995a; Vande Kopple, 2000). We also missed the opportunity to discuss how sub-disciplinary specialties may have different rhetorical needs and conventions/preferences that reflect those needs.

Example #2: Different Expectations about Titles

Titles in scientific research articles are also key elements, as readers frequently decide on the basis of the title and the abstract whether it is worthwhile to read the paper (Berkenkotter & Huckin, 1995a; Hyland, 2003). We said that the title should be "brief and informative"—and interpreted that instruction differently.

Our differences stemmed from unexpected results. The students were trying a new system for cloning a gene and expressing the protein, and the instructors did not know in advance if this approach would work. As it turned out, parts of it did, and parts of it didn't. The students then wanted to know how to represent this complicated situation in the title. The most informative answer is that part A worked but part B didn't, and I first advocated saying precisely that. However, Tip quickly brought up a complication: today, there is a clear preference for "positive results," or results that confirm one's expectation or hypothesis (Fanelli, 2012, p. 891). In addition, most scientists find reports of methods more interesting if the method actually works, as they want to know about possible improvements to their own methodology. Thus, Tip argued that students should make a hedged claim that emphasized the positive but with limits: the first part worked, while the second part worked minimally.

Once again, I found myself emphasizing agreement. We agreed that titles should be informative, and also that you should make the best possible case for something being interesting, and I emphasized that common ground. However, we *didn't* have the deeper conversation about when one might want to admit that something didn't work. When we discussed it later, it turned out that one consideration involved the difference between my and Tip's views on what genre and purposes the student laboratory reports were approximating. Were they approaching a very technical methods research paper (my thought), in which case it might be appropriate to say that something didn't work in order to save others from trying the same approach? Or were they approximating a research paper (her thought)—a paper that reports only after all difficulties have been ironed out?

In effect, this disagreement stemmed from a common issue in assignment design that we had not made explicit for the students. The lab report is frequently an artificial genre that reflects an attempt to teach at least two skills simultaneously during a laboratory course: the basics of the research report genre and the use of disciplinary technical protocols. It thus suffers from a serious internal complication: it uses the structure of a genuine research report while asking students to report on work that differs significantly from true investigation, in that it focuses on successfully replicating accepted knowledge and/or techniques (Moskovitz & Kellogg, 2011). This issue leads to at least two complexities. First, it makes for difficulties in writing the introduction, as the normal progression from known information to the question at hand requires that students pretend that the question has not already been answered. Second, it can confuse students about the true nature of research, as they are asked to evaluate their work on how well they replicated others' work, rather than finding and integrating something new.

We attempted to address at least the first issue by incorporating a relative unknown that is common in science: would the new system that has worked for similar tasks work in this particular situation? However, this choice created a new problem, as we continued to ask the students to write their introductory material as if they were framing a question about the biological process at hand rather than the technical details necessary to explore the biological process. The lab report instructions had, as Russell & Yañez (2003) put it, "strategic ambiguity" about this complication (p. 342), and students duly queried us. We helped them bridge the difference by instructing them to frame their question/purpose in these terms: "as a first step toward answering the interesting biological question, we need to first determine whether we can experimentally express the protein." However, this solution did not answer the question of which overlapping activity system with different motives they belonged to: one interested in technical details, or one interested in the biological process—and in fact could not, as we wanted them to be interested in both.

This reflection highlights the difficulties inherent in what Wardle (2009) calls "mutt genres" (p.765), or genres that use the forms that are authentic discursive tools in some activity systems but that fail to match the object and motives of the actual student activity system. By failing to follow up on our differences about titles, we missed an opportunity to discuss our mixed purposes and the difficulties inherent in the lab report genre, as well as how, in other situations, the same set of experiments could belong to two different activity systems, and thus be presented differently.

In addition, sub-disciplinary preferences for self-promotion may also have played a role in Tip's greater tendency to accentuate the positive. In a context when positive results are more highly valued, the desire to frame one's work in terms of the parts that worked is part of the promotional picture. Hyland (2003) noted disciplinary differences in the tendency to cite one's own work (a form of self-promotion). Similarly, Swales (2004) and Kanoksilapatham (2012) outlined disciplinary and sub-disciplinary preferences for explicitly promoting the importance of the work in the discussion sections. In addition, Fanelli (2010) directly addressed the question of disciplinary tendency to report a positive result, showing that the predisposition to report positive results correlates with one's position on the hard/soft and pure/applied axes. Additionally, in a comparison of four different biology sub-disciplines (Fanelli, 2010, 2012), she found important sub-disciplinary differences, although the magnitude of the difference depended on which time period she examined. In papers from 1990–2007, immunologists tended to be less likely to report positive results than molecular biologists (mirroring my preference); however, in papers from 2000–2007, immunologists were more likely to report positive results.

Taking all of this into account, Tip and I may be reflecting our different opinions about the particular activity system under consideration, our sub-disciplinary biases, or perhaps the age at which we first learned to write fluently as members of a scientific community. We might be also reflecting individual attitudes toward publication and self-promotion; many reviewers over the course of my career have said that I am too blunt. The truth may in fact be "all of the above." Regardless of the precise reasons, it is clear that, as with the figure legend situation, I lost the opportunity to engage my collaborator in a discussion that might show students how writing choices are driven by many interacting factors including rhetorical situation, sub-disciplinary norms, and individual preferences.

Engineering Teachable Moments

These examples show that my initial hunch contained elements of truth—sub-disciplinary expectations probably did influence our choices—but was incomplete in that it underestimated the effect of many other rhetorical considerations. What it really showed me was the importance of exploring and articulating the reasons for one's writing choices and sharing those reasons with students.

How might professors engage in this process and harness difference when teaching? I offer some suggestions to choose from that are probably most applicable to upper-level or capstone courses. These draw heavily on Bawarshi & Reiff's (2010) genre analysis recommendations, with an increased focus on designing the genre set and discussion of the rhetorical situation to highlight systematic sub-disciplinary differences, as well as on Thaiss & Zawacki's (2006) suggestions for making clear how classroom writing instructions reflect academic, disciplinary, sub-disciplinary, institutional, and personal exigencies.

During preparation:

1. *Examine genre variations within your discipline.* Actively look for areas of disagreement within your discipline. Compare your writing and your colleague's, and discuss: how are your writing choices different from your colleague's? To what do you attribute this difference? Examine the instructions for authors from journals that you publish in, and compare to the instructions in your colleagues' journals. What can this tell you about the relationship between sub-discipline and genre usage? Consider whether or how to include this knowledge in your teaching. For instance, can you represent different sub-disciplines through readings or explicit mentions during activities?

2. *Explore how rhetorical purpose changes the basic genre forms.* Actively consider how the rhetorical purpose affects form. For instance, a research article meant to highlight a minor improvement in methodology can be very different from one meant to answer to a gap in the literature. If your writing assignment only approximates a specialist genre, consider how the approximation will affect rhetorical choices within the genre, or how you might achieve the same learning goals with a more authentic writing task (Bean, 2011).

While teaching:

3. *Assign explicit rhetorical genre analysis.* Before the first draft of your writing assignment, ask students to do genre analysis (Swales 1990, 2004) and compare their analyses with their peers'. (This would have made sense as preparation for our second workshop on the IMRD structure, and might have made the third workshop unnecessary.) Resist the urge to assign samples that fit some mental ideal and instead actively look for differences to explore. If your course includes papers from a wide time period, consider having students explore differences over time. If it includes a range of sub-disciplines, select journals representing these overlapping specialties, give students a little information about the areas, and then ask them to see if they can identify which elements seem to be common and which vary depending on sub-discipline. This approach, growing out of the extensive

body of literature on genre analysis, is a potential point of contact with first-year composition (FYC), especially if FYC has been taught with a comparative genre analysis approach (Wolfe, Olson, & Wilder, 2014).

4. *Assign reflection about how choice relates to discipline or sub-discipline.* If students originally write the report targeted to a particular disciplinary or sub-disciplinary community, have them include a reflection describing what they learned during genre analysis about the (sub-)disciplinary community to which it was targeted, and what rhetorical choices they made within the overall framework to appeal to the community's particular needs and values. Or, ask students to re-write part of the report as if they were members of a second sub-discipline, and then have them reflect on what choices they had to make to appeal to the second audience.

5. *Map the discipline and its communicative practices.* If your departmental curriculum or course draws on multiple sub-disciplines, consider mapping the sub-disciplines for the student. Then ask them to reflect on the reading and writing tasks that they have been asked to do in other courses and note whether they can identify any sub-disciplinary differences. While this activity could take place as an extended discussion over a semester, using a writing-about-writing approach similar to one that might take place in a FYC course (Downs & Wardle, 2007), it could also work as a single workshop, especially if students are asked to do some genre analysis in preparation.

6. *Embrace disagreement.* If you are team-teaching, allow time to explore any differences that the students notice. In addition, encourage students to reflect on places where your suggestions sound contrary to something they have heard before. By all means, highlight any underlying areas of agreement—but don't "elide difference." Instead, explore the reasons for the difference, and try to articulate reasons that link to the rhetorical needs of the particular community in a particular time.

The above suggestions focus on what an individual instructor can do or what WID specialists might offer workshops on doing. It is also important to consider how these elements fit in with the overall curriculum. Student writers develop over their four years in college, and writing instruction—both at the level of FYC and in disciplinary writing—must consider how to facilitate writing transfer, or the ability to take skills from FYC and use them to develop greater facility with disciplinary writing (Beaufort, 2007; Bergmann & Zepernick, 2007; Driscoll, 2011; Nowacek, 2011; Wardle, 2009).

Based on the increasing recognition that students are having difficulty with transfer, the past decade has seen an increasing number of calls for development of *vertical curricula* for writing (Beaufort, 2007; Hall, 2006; Jamieson, 2009; Melzer, 2014;

Miles et al., 2008; Rhoades & Carroll, 2012; Smit, 2004; Yancey, Robertson, & Taczak, 2014). A vertical (or integrated or connected) curriculum considers what disciplinary reading and writing skills are desirable or required by graduation, and then designs a series of courses, starting with FYC and extending into the disciplines. Ideally, these courses should fully integrate the disciplinary content, sequence writing tasks appropriately, use consistent terminology for writing skills, and integrate metacognitive thinking about writing as well as peer feedback (Melzer, 2014).

While this is still an ideal rather than a widespread, fully integrated practice, some aspects of my experience may be applicable to the emerging design of such curricula. In particular, disciplinary departments might consider how different sub-disciplines are represented in their department and how the writing tasks and conventions differ within those sub-disciplines. Using this information, they can organize some writing instruction around discovering these differences and developing facility with discovering when one has entered a new disciplinary sub-community.

Acknowledgments

First, I want to thank my colleague and co-teacher, Dr. Cheeptip Benyajati, for many happy years teaching and learning together, as well as for her ideas that went into this paper and her thoughtful commentary on multiple drafts. I also thank Dr. Alexander Rosenberg for spot-checking the figure legend identifications and Drs. Jacqueline Cason, Rachel Lee, Sarah Perrault, Kathryn Phillips, and Deborah Rossen-Knill for helpful discussions and suggestions while I was developing this paper.

References

Bawarshi, A. S., & Reiff, M. J. (2010). Rhetorical genre studies approaches to teaching writing. In *Genre: An introduction to history, theory, research, and pedagogy* (pp. 189–209). West Lafayette, IN: Parlor Press.

Bazerman, C. (1984). Modern evolution of the experimental report in physics: Spectroscopic articles in Physical Review, 1893–1980. *Social Studies of Science, 14*(2), 163–96.

Bazerman, C. (1988). *Shaping written knowledge: The genre and activity of the experimental article in science.* Madison: University of Wisconsin Press.

Bean, J. C. (2011). *Engaging ideas: The professor's guide to integrating writing, critical thinking, and active learning in the classroom* (2nd ed.). SanFrancisco, CA: John Wiley & Sons.

Beaufort, A. (2007). *College writing and beyond.* Logan: Utah State University Press.

Becher, T., & Trowler, P. (2001). *Academic tribes and territories: Intellectual enquiry and the culture of disciplines.* Philadelphia, PA: Open University Press.

Benyajati, C. (2012). Laboratory in molecular, cellular, and developmental biology [classroom handout]. Department of Biology, University of Rochester, Rochester, NY.

Benyajati, C., Mueller, L., Xu, N., Pappano, M., Gao, J., Mosammaparast, M., . . . Elgin, S. (1997). Multiple isoforms of GAGA factor, a critical component of chromatin structure. *Nucleic Acids Research, 25*(16), 3345–53.

Bergmann, L. S., & Zepernick, J. (2007). Disciplinarity and transfer: Students' perceptions of learning to write. *WPA: Writing Program Administration, 31*(1–2), 124–49.

Berkenkotter, C., & Huckin, T. N. (1993). Rethinking genre from a sociocognitive perspective. *Written Communication, 10*(4), 475–509.

Berkenkotter, C., & Huckin, T. N. (1995a). News value in scientific journal articles. In *Genre knowledge in disciplinary communication: Cognition/culture/power* (pp. 27–44). Mahwah, NJ: Lawrence Erlbaum Associates, Inc.

Berkenkotter, C., & Huckin, T. N. (1995b). Rethinking genre from a sociocognitive perspective. In *Genre knowledge in disciplinary communication: Cognition/culture/power* (pp. 1–25). Mahwah, NJ: Lawrence Erlbaum Associates, Inc.

Biglan, A. (1973). The characteristics of subject matter in different academic areas. *Journal of Applied Psychology, 57*(3), 195–203.

Bizzell, P. (1992). What is a discourse community? In *Academic discourse and critical consciousness* (pp. 222–37). PA: University of Pittsburgh Press.

Culver, G. M., & Noller, H. F. (1999). Efficient reconstitution of functional Escherichia coli 30S ribosomal subunits from a complete set of recombinant small subunit ribosomal proteins. *RNA, 5*(6), 832–43.

Downs, D., & Wardle, E. (2007). Teaching about writing, righting misconceptions:(Re) envisioning "first-year composition" as "Introduction to Writing Studies." *College Composition and Communication, 58*(4), 552–84.

Driscoll, D. L. (2011). Connected, Disconnected, or Uncertain: Student Attitudes about Future Writing Contexts and Perceptions of Transfer from First Year Writing to the Disciplines. *Across the Disciplines, 8*(2). Retrieved from http://wac.colostate.edu/ATD/articles/drisco112011/index.cfm

Duff, P. A. (2010). Language socialization into academic discourse communities. *Annual Review of Applied Linguistics, 30*, 169–92.

Engeström, Y. (1987). Learning by expanding: An activity-theoretical approach to developmental research. In *XMCA Research Paper Archive*. Retrieved from: http://lchc.ucsd.edu/mca/Paper/Engestrom/Learning-by-Expanding.pdf

Fanelli, D. (2010). "Positive" results increase down the Hierarchy of the Sciences. *PloS one, 5*(3), 1–10. doi:10.1371/journal.pone.0010068

Fanelli, D. (2012). Negative results are disappearing from most disciplines and countries. *Scientometrics, 90*(3), 891–904.

Hall, J. (2006). Toward a unified writing curriculum: Integrating WAC/WID with freshman composition. *The WAC Journal, 17*, 5–22.

Hyland, K. (2003). Self-citation and self-reference: Credibility and promotion in academic publication. *Journal of the American Society for Information Science and Technology,* 54(3), 251–59.

Hyland, K. (2004a). Disciplinary cultures, texts, and interactions. In *Disciplinary discourses: Social interactions in academic writing* (pp. 1–19). Ann Arbor: University of Michigan Press.

Hyland, K. (2004b). *Disciplinary discourses: Social interactions in academic writing.* Ann Arbor: University of Michigan Press.

Hyland, K. (2005). Stance and engagement: A model of interaction in academic discourse. *Discourse Studies,* 7(2), 173–92.

Jamieson, S. (2009). The vertical writing curriculum. In J. C. Post and J. A. Inman (Eds.), *Composition(s) in the new liberal arts* (pp. 159–184). Creskill, NY: Hampton Press.

Kanoksilapatham, B. (2012). Research article structure of research article introductions in three engineering subdisciplines. *IEEE Transactions on Professional Communication,* 55(4), 294–309.

Kuhn, T. S. (1977). *The essential tension: Selected studies in scientific tradition and change.* IL: The University of Chicago Press.

Levin, S. A. (2006). Fundamental questions in biology. *PLoS Biology,* 4(9), 1471.

MacDonald, S. P. (1987). Problem definition in academic writing. *College English,* 49(3), 315–31.

Melzer, D. (2014). The connected curriculum: Designing a vertical transfer writing curriculum. *The WAC Journal,* 25, 78–90.

Miles, L., Pennell, M., Owens, K. H., Dyehouse, J., O'Grady, H., Reynolds, N., ... Shamoon, L. (2008). Thinking Vertically: Commenting on Douglas Downs and Elizabeth Wardle's "Teaching about Writing, Righting Misconceptions." *College Composition and Communication,* 59(3), 503–11.

Miller, C. R. (1984). Genre as social action. *Quarterly Journal of Speech,* 70(2), 151-167.

Moskovitz, C., & Kellogg, D. (2011). Science education. Inquiry-based writing in the laboratory course. *Science,* 332(6032), 919–20.

Nowacek, R. S. (2009). Why is being interdisciplinary so very hard to do? Thoughts on the perils and promise of interdisciplinary pedagogy. *College Composition and Communication,* 60(3), 493–516.

Nowacek, R. S. (2011). *Agents of integration: Understanding transfer as a rhetorical act.* Carbondale: Southern Illinois University Press.

Ozturk, I. (2007). The textual organisation of research article introductions in applied linguistics: Variability within a single discipline. *English for Specific Purposes,* 26(1), 25–38.

Petraglia, J. (1995). Writing as an unnatural act. In *Reconceiving writing, rethinking writing instruction* (pp. 79–100). Hillsdale, NY: Lawrence Erlbaum Associates.

Prior, P. (1995). Tracing authoritative and internally persuasive discourses: A case study of response, revision, and disciplinary enculturation. *Research in the Teaching of English, 29*(3), 288–325.

Prior, P. (1998). *Writing/disciplinarity: A sociohistoric account of literate activity in the academy.* Mahwah, NJ: Lawrence Erlbaum Associates.

Ramanathan, V., & Kaplan, R. B. (2000). Genres, authors, discourse communities: Theory and application for (L1 and) L2 writing instructors. *Journal of Second Language Writing, 9*(2), 171–91.

Rhoades, G., & Carroll, B. (2012). Supporting a Vertical Writing Model: Faculty Conversations Across the Curriculum. *Currents in Teaching & Learning, 4*(2), 42–50.

Roth, W.-M., & Lee, Y.-J. (2007). "Vygotsky's neglected legacy": Cultural-historical activity theory. *Review of Educational Research, 77*(2), 186–232.

Russell, D. (1995). Activity theory and its implications for writing instruction. In J. Petraglia (Ed.), *Reconceiving writing, rethinking writing instruction* (pp. 51–78). Hillsdale, NJ: Lawrence Erlbaum Associates.

Russell, D. R. (2002) *Writing in the academic disciplines: A curricular history.* Carbondale: Southern Illinois University Press.

Russell, D. R., & Yañez, A. (2003). "Big picture people rarely become historians": Genre systems and the contradictions of general education. In C. Bazerman & D. R. Russel (Eds.), *Writing selves/writing societies: Research from activity perspectives* (pp. 331–62). Fort Collins, CO: Wac Clearinghouse. Retrieved from http://wac.colostate.edu/books/selves_societies/.

Samraj, B. (2002). Introductions in research articles: Variations across disciplines. *English for Specific Purposes, 21*(1), 1–17.

Samraj, B. (2005). An exploration of a genre set: Research article abstracts and introductions in two disciplines. *English for Specific Purposes, 24*(2), 141–56.

Schaefer, K. L., & McClure, W. R. (1997). Antisense RNA control of gene expression in bacteriophage P22 .1. Structures of sar RNA and its target, ant mRNA. *RNA, 3*(2), 141–56.

Sia, E. A., Dominska, M., Stefanovic, L., & Petes, T. D. (2001). Isolation and characterization of point mutations in mismatch repair genes that destabilize microsatellites in yeast. *Molecular and Cellular Biology, 21*(23), 8157–67.

Smit, D. W. (2004). *The end of composition studies.* Carbondale: Southern Illinois University Press.

Swales, J. (1990). *Genre analysis: English in academic and research settings.* New York, NY: Cambridge University Press.

Swales, J. (2004). *Research genres: Explorations and applications.* New York, NY: Cambridge University Press.

Thaiss, C., & Zawacki, T. M. (2006). *Engaged writers and dynamic disciplines: Research on the academic writing life.* Portsmouth, NH: Boynton/Cook Publishers.

Toulmin, S. (1958). *The Uses of Argument*. Cambridge: Cambridge University Press.

Vande Kopple, W. J. (2000, April). *Dynamic and Synoptic Styles, Kinds of Semiotic Practices, and Learning To Write in the Disciplines*. Paper Presented at the Convention of the Conference on College Composition and Communication, Minneapolis, MN. Retrieved from http://eric.ed.gov/?id=ED442099.

Wardle, E. (2009). "Mutt Genres" and the goal of FYC: Can we help students write the genres of the university? *College Composition and Communication, 60*(4), 765–89.

Wolfe, J., Olson, B., & Wilder, L. (2014). Knowing what we know about Writing In the Disciplines: A new approach to teaching for transfer in FYC. *The WAC Journal, 25*, 42–77.

Yancey, K. B., Robertson, L., & Taczak, K. (2014). *Writing across contexts: Transfer, composition, and sites of writing*. Logan: Utah State University Press.

Cross-Curricular Consulting: How WAC Experts Can Practice Adult Learning Theory to Build Relationships with Disciplinary Faculty

DENISE ANN VRCHOTA

> So I've been toying with the idea of just going with groups of four and then I would have all the groups in both sections being the same size. So is that better or is it better to do an experiment where I've got one set in groups of three and one set with groups of four? Then, would they somehow be unhappy if, you know, if you were in one section and you were in a group of three but you could have been in the other section and been in a group of four?
>
> —Food Science Professor

These questions were posed by a food science professor who incorporates group assignments and laboratories into her courses in order for students to learn disciplinary content and to prepare them for professional practice. The query is similar to those of other faculty members who participated in the study reported here: disciplinary faculty members who carefully and deliberately integrated communication activities into their classes but whose primary expertise lay in their own discipline rather than in the discipline of communication studies, of which I am a part. My initial response to the professor's question was that among the decisions she would make as she developed the group activity, the number of students assigned to each group would not be the most pressing. Before I responded, however, there were two decisions I needed to make: first, whether to respond to her query or direct her to what I felt were more pressing group issues; and second, the best way to initiate whichever group issue I would decide to tackle first. I see similar dilemmas in the writing across the curriculum (WAC) literature where, for example, Cole (2014) points out that for WAC consultants, grammar is only a very small piece of the pie, while for disciplinary faculty members, it appears to be a very large piece. The issues in both of these scenarios are first, whether it is advisable to respond to priorities set by disciplinary faculty members or steer them to what the cross-curricular consultant views as more pressing priorities; and second, determining the best approach to managing the interaction. The present discussion is based on the assumption that neither cross-curricular consultants nor disciplinary faculty members have sufficient knowledge to remedy all disciplinary dilemmas. They must work together, discovering the assumptions that drive each, questioning the basis of those assumptions, and eventually arriving at a resolution based on the expertise each group brings to the table. In the examples given, both parties could clarify their assumptions about the role of issues important to them (such as grammar or group size) to the benefit of the other. The cross-curricular consultant might learn that what seems to him or her to be an inconsequential disciplinary issue assumes an important place in preparing students for professional practice. Similarly, the disciplinary faculty has an opportunity to learn that writing is more than grammar or that group work is more than seating individuals around a table.

Admittedly I am external to the work of WAC consultants, but I've learned much from reading the WAC research that is rich in strategies for writing consultants who work with what sometimes appear to be a "close-minded [disciplinary] faculty" (Jablonski, 2006). I've also identified areas in the WAC research where my expertise in communication might be useful to WAC consultants, and in this discussion I will share one main area where WAC and CXC might have mutual interests: adult learning theory. But first I want to note the shared challenges to which adult learning theory might speak. As a member of the communication studies discipline, I also work with faculty members in other disciplines to support their efforts, and as a communication across the curriculum (CXC) consultant, I help them develop presentation assignments and group and interpersonal communication activities. Although there are differences in written communication and oral communication (Vrchota and Russell, 2013), our disciplines are branches on the same family tree (both grew out of rhetoric, though they parted ways one hundred years ago in 1915), and for both writing and communication experts, our work with members of other disciplines is an increasingly important part of what our disciplines do. My reading of the WAC research indicates that we also share similar challenges as we work with disciplinary faculty members. In particular, there are two common areas of concern where I will suggest a communication approach to working with disciplinary faculty members: the challenges of building professional relationships with disciplinary faculty members and the need to develop a common foundation upon which to conduct our work. Although it is possible that WAC consultants already practice some or all of the communication approaches I will suggest, perhaps by theorizing them it may be possible to consult more consciously and mindfully and to be aware when one is not practicing these approaches.

First, the challenge of building professional relationships with disciplinary faculty members, which is experienced by communication consultants and which is also discussed in the WAC research, may be more onerous for WAC consultants. In WAC literature, the resistance of disciplinary faculty members is attributed to reasons such as a lack of training about writing, the view that writing assignments and their subsequent grading are time-consuming and detract from more important disciplinary activities, and the view that writing is drudgery because it is about uninteresting activities like grammar, or other areas that appear to have no tangible or immediate outcome (Cole, 2014; Jablonski, 2006; Rodrigue, 2012; Ronesi, 2011; Rutz & Grawe, 2009; Stout, 2011; Tarabochia, 2013). WAC consultants may, at times, perceive that disciplinary faculty members view them as "coercive, manipulative, and controlling" (Donahue, 2002, p. 35), causing disciplinary faculty members to avoid them, ignore their efforts to reach out, and "refuse to make eye contact" (Donahue, 2002, p. 34).

The second challenge shared by communication and WAC consultants is the need to build a foundation upon which consultants and disciplinary faculty members can work together, honoring both their own and the other's disciplinary traditions. This second challenge may also be more pressing for WAC than for communication consultants due to the fact that discussions of communication are sometimes lost among other details of an assignment or classroom activity, whereas a written text is a visible entity, perhaps making it more distinct. Several possible solutions have been offered in WAC literature, such as a shared meta-language for talking about writing in an effort to provide a common basis to facilitate WAC and disciplinary faculty interaction (Melzer, 2014). Others advocate the development of standardized tools such as university-wide rubrics (Bohr & Rhoades, 2014; Cole, 2014). Another group of WAC consultants calls for cross-curricular consulting approaches that honor differing writing traditions specific to individual disciplines and acknowledge faculty freedom of choice to implement suggestions that come from writing experts. Writing experts who support this approach cite the necessity of speaking the language of disciplinary counterparts (Allan, 2013; Anson & Dannels, 2009; Bohr & Rhodes, 2014; Cole, 2014; Paretti, 2011; Robinson & Hall, 2013; Rutz & Grawe, 2009; Soliday, 2011; Tarabochia, 2013; Walvoord, Hunt, Dowling, & McMahon, 1997; Wolfe, Olson, & Wilder, 2014.) These concerns resonate with CXC research and theory (See for example, Dannels, 2000, 2001, 2002, 2003, 2005; Dannels, Anson, Bullard, & Peretti, 2003; Dannels, Gaffney, & Martin, 2008; Dannels & Norris Martin, 2008; Darling & Dannels, 2003).

Of course, despite these shared challenges, neither WAC nor communication consultants have become so discouraged as to give up their efforts to provide assistance to their colleagues in the disciplines and have developed numerous strategies intended to overcome disciplinary faculty resistance, recognizing that "it's difficult to collaborate even though we know it's important" (Tarabouchia, 2013). The overarching need of both WAC and communication consultants is to find a way for us to utilize our expertise in a manner that will be recognized and valued by disciplinary faculty members. For much of my career, I have worked with faculty members in other disciplines, assisting them to develop communication activities for their classes.

I also conduct qualitative research in order to learn more about the integral connection between communication and disciplinary traditions that, in turn, helps me to provide more useful assistance to the faculty (see, for example, Reitmeier, Svendsen, & Vrchota, 2004; Reitmeier & Vrchota, 2009; Vrchota, 2015a, 2015b, 2012, 2011; Vrchota & Russell, 2013). Since 2000 I have worked with faculty members in three pre-professional programs, all housed in a food science department. The programs are dietetics, food science, and nutrition; each program studies food, but the focus of each differs. What I have found to be vastly different across the three programs is the connection of communication traditions to the disciplinary content of each: in dietetics, interpersonal communication is crucial in order to conduct patient interviews; in food science, most work in the food industry occurs in groups; in nutrition, presentation competencies are key to disseminate research at professional meetings and to secure funding. I will use qualitative examples from the data I collected while working with faculty members in these three programs in order to illustrate the consulting approach I promote in the present discussion.

In all of this work, the most helpful set of tools I have found are from the field of adult learning theory. It has guided my overall approach to disciplinary faculty members. As cross-curricular consultants, we know our relationships with disciplinary faculty members are potentially perilous, often because of the very reasons we are working together: e.g., our disciplinary roles and our own disciplinary traditions. Jablonski (2006) described the interaction between disciplinary faculty members and cross-curricular consultants as much more complex than "brown bag lunch" collaborations (p. 12). Despite the complexity of our relationships and our disciplinary influences, at our cores, as Donahue (2002) observed, faculty members are adults, and cross-curricular experts are teachers who are teaching adult teachers. It is our core identities as adults that ground the suggestions I make about relationship-building with disciplinary faculty; these suggestions are framed by two prominent adult learning theories: andragogy (Knowles, 1980) and transformational learning theory (TLT) (Mezirow, 2000).

Similarly, the application of concepts from my own discipline to relationship-building with disciplinary faculty members is crucial if I wish to make any progress with them. In the following sections I provide more specific information about communication competencies useful to cross-curricular consultants as they build relationships with disciplinary faculty.

Finally, Tarabochia (2013) observed that "writing specialists need strategies for communicating across disciplinary differences" because of "the unique intersection of disciplinary difference, ideologies, epistemologies, value-based principles, and objectives (among other forces) shaping the interactions." In communication studies, there is a situated framework (Dannels, 2001) that acknowledges the integral connection between communication and a discipline, a connection that guides cross-curricular consultants to identify the framework of disciplinary oral discourse. I will suggest questions based on this situated framework that may be useful to writing consultants in understanding other disciplinary traditions and in creating those integral connections.

Conducting Cross-Curricular Consulting with Adult Learning Theories

Two prominent adult learning theories provide guidance for building the consultant-faculty relationship: andragogy (Knowles, 1980), which defines adults as particular kinds of learners within a learning context, and transformational learning theory (TLT) (Mezirow, 2000), which describes the qualities of an adult learning relationship and the roles of the individuals within it.

According to andragogy, adults are defined as self-directed individuals who prefer to partner in their own learning; they possess a repertoire of life (professional) experiences and, on the basis of these experiences, they know what they need or want to learn—they are problem-solvers who seek immediate applications to solve their problems. When I began consulting with the three programs, communication activities designed for the purposes of meeting accreditation mandates and preparing students for professional practice in their respective areas of study were already part of many classes. When the activities fell short of providing the experiences for students that the faculty members anticipated, they asked me to suggest modifications in response to the flaws they perceived in those activities so that they could meet accreditation mandates and provide more valuable professional preparation for students.

The characteristics andragogy attributes to adults explain the varying degrees of receptiveness with which disciplinary faculty members respond to consultants' suggestions. For WAC consultants, for example, andragogy would propose that the apparent preoccupation that disciplinary faculty members show regarding grammar, described in WAC literature (Cole, 2014; Peretti, 2011; Rodrigue, 2012), is unlikely to disappear on its own; grammar needs to be dealt with if it is the issue the faculty members conclude they need to understand and view as a problem that needs a solution. The focus of andragogy on the qualities of self-directedness and the need for adults to partner in their own learning implies a relationship of equality, calling for cross-curricular consultants and disciplinary faculty members to seek solutions together rather than through what is sometimes described as a doctor-patient relationship (Schein, 1987), an arrangement in which the doctor (cross-curricular consultant) diagnoses the problem and tells the patient (disciplinary faculty member) what to do about it.

TLT supports andragogy by proposing that adults in learning contexts acquire the knowledge they need by disclosing to others the assumptions upon which they base their actions. According to TLT, learning is the result of dialogue where the participating parties are "trying on another's point of view" (Mezirow, 2000, p.21) as they express and test their own and the other's assumptions in order to arrive at a common understanding (Mezirow, 2003). This theory seems particularly apt for the cross-curricular consulting context, where each participant, the disciplinary faculty member and the cross-curricular consultant, is an expert in his or her own discipline but must learn about the assumptions that are the basis of the other's discipline before both participants can work to meet the disciplinary faculty member's need. For example, I needed to understand the disciplinary assumptions that guide the patient interviews so crucial to the work of dietitians. Similarly, dietetics faculty members need to know the assumptions upon which interpersonal communication is based in order to understand why my suggestions might help them. What TLT does not address is the means by which the interactants proceed in order to acquire knowledge of the other's assumptions; that means is suggested by some principles drawn from communication theory and research, which I will turn to next.

Testing Assumptions and Communicating Across Disciplines

The approach proposed by TLT of expressing and testing assumptions is consistent with definitions of human communication, defined as: "making sense out of the world and attempting to share that sense with others" (Beebe, Beebe, & Redmond, 2014, p. 3). The communication competencies relevant to the consulting context originate in interpersonal communication, often described as face-to-face communication, where individuals concurrently send and receive messages through verbal and nonverbal channels with the goal of achieving common understanding, a goal in concert with TLT. The specific interpersonal competencies that I find most relevant to the exchange of assumptions necessary for both andragogy and transformational learning theory are empathic listening and psychological immediacy.

Empathic Listening

Cuny et al. (2012) advocate empathic listening as a means of building relationships at communication centers where staff members interact with individuals from differing disciplines; these relationships require "an active level of listening" (p. 249) so that staff members may understand the assumptions and needs of their clients. The relationship of communication-center staff members and their clients is similar to that between cross-curricular consultants and disciplinary faculty members. The model of empathic listening includes being attentive to the other, encouraging the other's words and ideas, and reflecting on the other's perspective and goals achieved through the following: 1) questioning, 2) paraphrasing, and 3) responding.

Questions are invaluable for initiating and conducting a cross-curricular consultation in order to learn the assumptions upon which the disciplinary faculty is operating and to build a foundation that allows consultants to communicate across disciplinary differences. There are specific questions that cross-curricular consultants can ask that will enable them to understand the connection between their expertise and the discipline within which they are working, based on Dannels' situated framework (2001). Dannels credits the work of writing specialists such as Bazerman (1997), Herrington (1985), and Winsor (1999) with the inspiration to develop a situated framework that theorizes the nature of oral communication in the disciplines. The framework proposes communication as a context-driven activity where oral genres are sites for disciplinary learning, oral argument is a situated practice, and standards for oral competence are generated within the discipline. The view is consistent with recent proposals by writing specialists (Blakeslee, Hayes, & Young, 1994; Hall & Hughes, 2011; Hansen & Adams, 2010; Walvoord, Hunt, Dowling, & McMahon, 1997), all of whom agree about the need to offer assistance to disciplinary faculty members in ways that integrate writing into courses while honoring disciplinary traditions. I suggest four questions, corresponding to the tenants of the situated framework, that are useful to learn about the connection between communication (and writing) and the discipline:

1. What communication (writing) activities do you include in your classes? What is your purpose for including these activities?

2. What are the communication (writing) activities in which students must be competent for professional practice? How do you prepare students for these activities?

3. What do you expect of students as they engage in these activities and how do you know whether they've met your expectations?

4. What are your concerns about developing and implementing communication (writing) activities? What support can I provide that would be helpful to you?

The responses to questions one and two result in information about the connection between communication (writing) and the discipline. In pre-professional programs, such as those described in the present discussion, the answers to these two questions often overlap. For example, one food science laboratory activity required students to take samples from food processing equipment and identify the proper tests to be used to determine bacteria levels. The assignment afforded practice in reviewing various food testing protocols and also applied to professional practices in the food industry where maintaining sanitary food processing equipment is crucial. When the instructor described the activity, I was prompted to ask whether professionals work alone, in pairs, or in groups or teams to conduct the testing. This led to suggestions to incorporate additional group competencies into the laboratory activity. The responses to these questions may also be enlightening to the instructor. A faculty member who taught a dietetics course online responded to question one by describing expectations that students should conduct their e-mail communications observing professional writing protocol. When I asked question two, I also asked if the e-mail expectations were part of the interpersonal communication competencies dietetics students were expected to acquire. The startled response was: "No, I don't even cover that. Isn't that crazy?"

Questions three and four are useful to understand the faculty member's knowledge of communication—or writing—and to preview the nature of the work the consultant may be called upon to provide in the discipline. I noticed the faculty would often not admit their uncertainties about communication, but their responses to question three on assessment procedures provided an avenue for them to express concerns that indirectly revealed a need for additional information. For example, one faculty member stated a concern about group activities: "I want to give better examples of things I would like the [peer] evaluators to say. Not just 'good job.'" Using empathic listening, I concluded the concern indicated an area about which the faculty might not know, which enabled me to address the concern and also give additional information about groups.

The response to the fourth question is a more direct indication of faculty questions and needs. One dietetics faculty member explained her need for time in order to integrate additional interview assignments that would prepare students to communicate with patients and health care professionals. I suggested developing a stock interview assignment to familiarize students with interview basics. Rather than participating in five interview role-plays with five different individuals, students would participate in one interview role-play and write or discuss brief descriptions of ways the basic interview would be modified to interact with patients and health care professionals.

Although I do not have a specific script of questions to be used for testing assumptions and for engaging in empathic listening, from communication studies come general suggestions about questioning. An examination of my interview transcripts reveals several goals that motivated the questions I asked faculty: to unearth the assumptions that undergird the goals of the discipline and the faculty ("What are the contexts within which a nutritionist would give a presentation?"); to make suggestions to faculty in a nonthreatening manner ("Would it be useful to hear some ideas about responding to a patient's unwillingness to disclose?"); to support consultants' suggestions in ways that make faculty resistance difficult ("Since you are concerned about the class time consumed by lengthy presentations, should we talk about ways to meet your assignment goals with reduced time requirements?). Questions facilitate consultants' learning what they need to know in order to offer useful advice and provide a grounding with the disciplinary faculty.

One thing I have found is that faculty members tend to express concerns as part of their narration rather than asking questions, further emphasizing the importance of empathic listening. For example, the dietetics profession is increasingly concerned about professional dietitians' reticence to communicate with medical doctors and other health care professionals. One dietetics instructor designed a role-play, the goal of which was to reduce the reticence. Her descriptions of students' responses—"they laughed, they giggled, they thought it was funny that they should have to practice this . . ."—is probably a means of asking for suggestions for ways to encourage students to respond to the assignment more seriously. That is my cue to find out the nature of the help needed: "What was the goal of the assignment?" or "How did you introduce the assignment?"

One piece of advice about questions: order your questions so that you aren't asking those with a limited response range too soon. Introducing the conversation with a question to which there are few possible responses ("How many writing—or speaking—assignments do you give your students?") potentially limits the content of the response and, as a result, crucial information might not be revealed. Start with the big questions first. "What are your most effective communication (writing) assignments?" will give you hints about follow-up questions you didn't even know you should ask, the answers to which are likely to be useful to you in learning disciplinary assumptions.

Questions identify assumptions, but once assumptions have been identified, paraphrasing serves other important functions: first, paraphrasing checks the accuracy of your interpretation of what was said. Since you are working with faculty members from another discipline, the terminology or disciplinary definitions of your disciplines may differ. A nutrition instructor and I talked at length about presentations. Early paraphrasing on my part would have clarified that one of us was referring to public speaking and the other to nonverbal communication. A second reason to paraphrase is to check your understanding of disciplinary traditions. For instance, when a food science instructor expressed concern about students who described food products in personal terms—"Yum, I like it"—I responded with "You are saying that students cannot express whether they like the foods they make." My paraphrase of what I thought was the instructor's point gave her the opportunity to explain that students are expected to learn and use food science terminology to describe their responses rather than to respond personally. Third, by paraphrasing, you are giving the other individual an opportunity to reflect on the logic or accuracy of his or her thought: "You're saying that the fixed seating in your room prohibits you from having group activities" prompted the instructor to consider whether that was the real reason he avoided group activities. Finally, paraphrasing provides an entry to make a suggestion from the perspective of the disciplinary faculty. To a nutrition instructor who felt she did not have the time to prepare students for a major presentation, my paraphrase was the following: "The students present complex proposals to the class for which you are unable to provide preparation and you've indicated some concerns about the quality of the proposals. I suggest . . . ."

The third area of empathic listening is making suggestions. The cross-curricular consultant's response to the concerns the disciplinary faculty member has implicitly or explicitly voiced may become a risky action for either party. Dannels (2010) describes disciplinary faculty members who dare to teach subjects other than their own as risk-takers who are willing to step outside of the comfort zones of their own disciplines, and this risk is exacerbated when faculty concerns become public through their disclosure to cross-curricular experts. Taylor (2000) observes the disclosure resulting from the TLT approach can be painful, containing moments when both parties may feel they are losing or acquiescing in some way to accommodate the other. The cross-curricular consultant is also engaged in risk-taking by suggesting a course of action that may be ignored or criticized. In order for both parties to save face, I have found disciplinary faculty members to be more receptive to suggestions that are phrased tentatively rather than as unequivocal statements. Suggestions expressed tentatively also leave the door open for additional discussion. Also if there is resistance to the suggestion, the consultant can always fall back on "it was just a suggestion." Here are methods for phrasing suggestions in a tentative manner:

1. Base suggestions on disclosures from the disciplinary faculty: "You indicated uncertainty (concern, etc.) about _____. One thing you might try in that situation is_____."

2. Present suggestions as questions: "I wonder if you've considered trying _____?"

3. Ask permission to give suggestions: "I have an idea. Is this a good time to bring it up?"

4. Explain the reasoning for your suggestion: "In writing (communication), we have found that _____. There are similarities to your class, so you might want to try that."

5. Create empathy by admitting a similar dilemma and giving the solution that worked for you: "That same thing happens in my classes, so I do this: _____. It seems to work."

Psychological Immediacy

Empathic listening allows disciplinary faculty members and cross-curricular consultants to reveal the assumptions that drive their respective courses of action. But the efforts that go into the verbal exchange of assumptions will be most successful if accompanied by strategies to create psychological immediacy, a sense of psychological closeness (Mehrabian, 1981). Both verbal and nonverbal methods are recognized as ways to reduce distance and increase psychological immediacy (Witt & Wheeless, 2001). Verbally, immediacy is achieved through such approaches as use of inclusive pronouns ("we" vs. "I"); active verbs ("I'm working with you..." vs. "I've been asked to work with you..."); expressions of concern ("I want you to feel more confident about..." vs. "Students need to understand..."); and addressing by name ("John, how do you feel about...?" vs. "How do you feel about...?'). Nonverbally, immediacy is attained through displays such as frequent eye contact, relaxed posture, relevant and animated gestures and facial expression, and vocal variety (Mehrabian, 1981). Research in classroom settings has shown that high levels of verbal and nonverbal immediacy on the part of the instructor resulted in higher affect with students. Similarly, I've found that disciplinary faculty members are more receptive and involved in the consulting process if I display nonverbal actions that contribute to immediacy. I meet with faculty members in locations of their choice, usually their offices, because the comfort of talking within their own territories seems to reduce the threat of disclosing their concerns. I try not to take too many notes—for long-term consulting I tape conversations if faculty members agree—so I can be free to respond to their disclosures with appropriate facial and vocal expression. When relevant, I work to control my facial and vocal expression to mask signs of disapproval (or horror) because I don't want to come across as rigid or disapproving. I also nod to offer encouragement and support, and I maintain eye contact.

The interpersonal communication concepts presented here, empathic listening and psychological immediacy, work to enable the cross-curricular consultant to initiate and cultivate a relationship with disciplinary faculty members in order to gain information about the faculty and the disciplinary context so as to be most helpful. TLT identifies both participants, cross-curricular consultant and disciplinary faculty member, as learners and educators. The cross-curricular consultant learns about the disciplinary traditions of the faculty member in order to provide assistance to the faculty, while the disciplinary faculty member learns from the expertise of the cross-curricular consultant as he or she reveals information about the discipline. Both reflect on their own assumptions, and each may have those assumptions questioned by the other.

The adult learning theories upon which the present discussion is based frame the relationship of the disciplinary faculty member and cross-curricular consultant as one of equal engagement in learning; however, operating within this framework does not relieve the consultant of obligations he or she maintains as part of the consulting role. There are several general observations that I offer regarding specific situations that may emerge within the framework of adult learning theory. First, the cross curricular consultant should respond to inaccurate assumptions of faculty members when those assumptions interfere with faculty members reaching a disciplinary goal.

One nutrition instructor assumed all students in the class should provide peer feedback for every other classmate's presentation but was unable to reconcile the time the feedback took from other class activities and considered dropping the feedback activity. I suggested the instructor have students give feedback on a rotating schedule; that is, for each speech, a limited number of students would be designated to give feedback to each speaker or, alternatively, would be the feedback designees on a given day. The instructor took my suggestion without having to sacrifice students' opportunities to learn from the feedback or from other class activities.

Second, understand that the exchange of assumptions places both the disciplinary faculty member and the cross-curricular consultant in the role of learner. When the consultant accepts the role of learner, he or she may be more empathic about receiving information from the faculty member, which, in turn, should enhance the value of the suggestions given. Early in my work with the food scientists, the instructors in a food laboratory gave students a food testing assignment for which they would work in groups. I questioned the instructors' reasons for placing the students in groups that seemed very contrived rather than having the students conduct the testing individually. Their first response was to laugh and reply, "Because you told us [in a previous conversation]." They went on to explain:

> Very rarely do they [students] do things individually [in professional contexts]. In the food science discipline, it's more important maybe than in other disciplines [to be able to work in groups]. People in food science, you have to really work together. And it's extremely important for the students.

Learning about the privileged role of groups became an important factor in the development of many of the communication activities with faculty in the food science discipline and affirmed the crucial need for cross-curricular consultants to learn about the disciplines in which they work.

Third, know that you won't always make the sale. At times, cross-curricular consultants may need to quit pushing no matter how logical or evidence-based their suggestions are because faculty members just aren't interested. A nutrition instructor offered students the opportunity to present a short speech summarizing a lecture in order to earn extra-credit points while emphasizing that giving the extra-credit points was the purpose of the activity: he was "not nearly as concerned about the presentation, per se, the mechanics of it." At the same time, he was dissatisfied that the students' summaries were so detailed as to verge on transcripts of the lectures. I offered to help the instructor develop a brief guide to assist the students in generating the summaries he had in mind, assuming that if more attention were paid to the mechanics of the assignments, the students could still receive the extra-credit points, and, in the process, have an opportunity to practice their presentation (and writing) skills. In response, the instructor replied, "Your question has made me just sit here and think, 'what is my goal of that?' And I would have to say, it's probably the points." Should I have forced the issue? Although the activity was a perfect way to reinforce important disciplinary knowledge and, without a great deal of effort, provide the opportunity for students to practice speaking, that wasn't the instructor's priority. The lesson I learned is that understanding the other's assumptions signals the point at which to stop.

Fourth, anticipate faculty frustration about a lack of control over student outcomes on communication (and perhaps also writing) assignments. A food science instructor complained, "All this group stuff takes more time. It [the group activity] never reached the conclusion that I thought we were going to get to. When will they learn this idea?" In some disciplines, the dominant pedagogy of the discipline is lecture, with students assessed through quizzes or examinations, allowing faculty a high degree of control. When students engage in communication activities, the act of communicating also becomes the pedagogy (perhaps the same thing occurs when students engage in writing assignments), which makes it difficult to guide students to arriving at a specific answer. In instances such as this, knowing the assumptions of the faculty is paramount in order to help them, particularly knowing the instructor's learning goal. When the learning goal is for students to acquire disciplinary facts or procedural knowledge, lecture may be the best pedagogy. If the learning goal is for students to apply the factual or procedural knowledge to circumstances Huba and Freed (2000) name "ill-defined problems"—that is, disciplinary problems that "cannot be resolved with a high degree of certainty" (p. 203)—a communication (or writing) activity may be the best approach. Ascertaining the purpose of an activity is crucial.

Finally, there are times when the planets line up almost perfectly and the sharing of assumptions results in an outcome that gives satisfaction to both cross-curricular consultant and disciplinary faculty member. One such experience occurred with a dietetics instructor who wanted help developing a protocol for site visits with dietetics interns. The individual was just out of graduate school and struggling with the discrepancy between what she had been told about the goals of the site visits by more experienced faculty members and what she had noticed herself. On the basis of my own assumptions, I anticipated discussing interview competencies. The dietetics instructor's assumptions were vastly different. She described interns reporting feeling physically ill as they anticipated their site visits; site visits occurring without privacy in busy hospital hallways, making each interaction and constructive feedback difficult while also adding to the interns' anxiety; and a tradition dictating that interns were to discuss charts of patients they'd never seen before, which resulted in interns overlooking important notations due to their lack of familiarity with the cases. After I learned about the circumstances of the supervisory role from the dietetics instructor's perspective, my question was, "When your site visit is completed, what do you want accomplished?" Her stated goals were to create an environment where interns were not physically ill; to implement roles in which she and the interns were partners in learning; and to eliminate the tradition of unfamiliar charts—however, her goals resulted in uncertainty about how to conduct the site visit. The conversation went like this:

> Me: And if they've already reviewed the chart, they would know something about the patient.
>
> Her: And I could say "tell me about the patient."
>
> Me: What comes after "tell me about the patient"; what do you expect?
>
> Her (thoughtfully): "Tell me about the patient." That would include things like their diagnosis, their lifestyle, medications they're on [she continued to describe the details she would expect]. Well and also, if there's something I'm not real clear on, if there is the opportunity, typically they have a few resources with them, then I could say "Well, let's see what we can find about this."
>
> Me: That's excellent. You're learning together. It's good to show that we always have learning to do.

There are both advantages and disadvantages to applying TLT to cross-curricular consulting. Advantages include comparing assumptions that provide the disciplinary faculty and the cross-curricular consultant with a common perspective from which problems can be tackled and learning the motivations of the disciplinary faculty in order to make suggestions that resonate with those motivations. Revealing the assumptions that guide cross-curricular consultants in their recommendations can be similarly informative to disciplinary faculty members. A dietetics instructor was hesitant to give constructive feedback to dietetic interns who she felt had not effectively consulted with cardiac patients. My response to the concern was that the feedback was just as instrumental in cultivating professional interviewing competencies as was the experience itself. The instructor thought about my remark and began to describe her own experiences where she benefitted from receiving feedback.

The major disadvantage of framing cross-curricular consulting work in TLT is the time-consuming nature of the activity. Sharing and exploring each other's assumptions is beneficial to the consulting outcome and to building a professional relationship, but for short-term consulting, TLT may be impractical. A second disadvantage pertains to the frustration that can result when the consultant's advice is ignored. My sense from reading the WAC literature is that writing consultants sometimes become frustrated when disciplinary faculty members choose not to implement their expert suggestions, a frustration I've also experienced when working with disciplinary faculty members. Aside from experiencing the frustration of resistance, there is also the issue of the extent to which adults can or should influence other adults. I try to remember that I am invited into the discipline as a consultant only; I have no official capacity. I work to make a logical case for my suggestions and then go on to the next issue. Obviously, I want to make a difference in the way disciplinary faculty members develop and implement communication activities in their classes, but I also don't want to appear so rigid that my effectiveness is reduced.

Implications for Future Research

The purpose of this discussion is to respond to two concerns shared by WAC and communication cross-curricular consultants. Adult learning theory was proposed as a framework for relationship-building between disciplinary faculty members and cross curricular consultants; empathic listening and psychological immediacy were suggested to manage and share assumptions and communicate across disciplinary differences. As I formulated the suggestions above, two issues have emerged for me for future discussion and research that I hope will be taken up by WAC faculty members who engage in cross-curricular consulting.

First, are the proposals for cross-curricular consulting contained in the present discussion applicable to *WAC cross-curricular consultations*? One of the shared needs of WAC and communication consultants identified in the present discussion was "strategies for communicating across disciplinary differences" (Tarabochia, 2013). To what extent, if at all, does a cross-curricular consulting strategy that works for one discipline also accommodate the consulting of another discipline? The adult learning framework that was the basis of the present discussion advocates relationship-building and the exchange of assumptions while working toward a shared meaning, which are also foundations of the communication discipline. For me, I am in my disciplinary home with this approach. But is the cross-curricular consulting repertoire for one discipline a good fit for the consulting repertoire of another discipline due to the very foundations upon which that discipline is built? I sincerely urge WAC consultants to apply some or all of the ideas proposed in this discussion to their cross-curricular consulting experiences and write their own accounts of the subsequent outcomes.

Second, are the proposals for cross-curricular consulting contained in the present discussion applicable to the *disciplinary content* of WAC cross-curricular consultations? The purpose of consultants and disciplinary faculty members sharing the assumptions of their disciplines is to negotiate an outcome that will meet the needs of the discipline, a process that may result in modification of the principles of the consulting discipline. Communication concepts and principles are contextually situated, lending flexibility to their application in other disciplines. Is the writing discipline similarly able to modify its principles and concepts to the needs of other disciplines? May the format or content of a memo be modified to fit disciplinary needs?

The resulting knowledge we gain from cross-curricular consulting benefits our consulting work and our disciplines by focusing on a place that Gallison (as cited in Huber & Morreale, 2002, pp. 2–3) referred to as "the trading zone," that borderland populated by scholars of collaborating disciplines. Our work as cross-curricular consultants affords us insights about our own discipline based on the reflections we receive from those with whom we consult.

Note

Quotations and examples inserted in the discussion to illustrate the approaches I've advocated for working with disciplinary faculty members are taken directly from transcripts of my interviews with faculty and from my field notes and other research data. All research reported in this discussion was collected after receiving approval from the local institutional review board.

References

Allan, E. G. (2013). Multi-modal rhetorics in the disciplines: Available means of persuasion in an undergraduate architectural studio. *Across the Disciplines, 10*(2). Retrieved from http://wac.colostate.edu/atd/articles/allan2013.cfm

Anson, C. A. & Dannels, D.P. (2009). Profiling programs: Formative uses of departmental consultations in the assessment of communication across the curriculum. *Across the Disciplines, 6*. Retrieved from http://wac.colostate.edu/atd/assessment/anson_dannels.cfm

Bazerman, C. (1997). Discursively structured activities. *Mind, Culture, and Activity, 4*, 293–308.

Beebe, S.A., Beebe, S. J., & Redmond, M. V. (2014). *Interpersonal communication: Relating to others* (7th ed.). Boston, MA: Pearson.

Blakeslee, A., Hayes, J., & Young, R. (1994). Evaluating training workshops in a writing across the curriculum program: method and analysis. *Language and Learning Across the Disciplines, 1*, 5–34. Retrieved from wac.colostate.edu/llad/vln2/blakeslee/pdf

Bohr, D. J. & Rhoades, G. (2014). The WAC glossary project: Facilitative conversations between composition and WID faculty in a unified writing curriculum. *Across the Disciplines, 11*(1). Retrieved from wac.colostate.edu/atd/articles/bohr_rhoades2014.cfm

Cole, D. (2014). What if the earth is flat? Working with, not against, faculty concerns about grammar in student writing. *The WAC Journal, 25*, 7–35. Retrieved from wac.colostate.edu/journal/vol25/cole.pdf

Cuny, K.M., Wilde, S. M., & Stephenson, A.V. (2012). Using empathic listening to build client relationships at the center. In E.L.Yook & W. Atkins-Sayre (Eds.), *Communication centers and oral communication programs in higher education* (pp.249–56). Lanham, MD: Lexington Books.

Dannels, D.P. (2000). Learning to be professional: Technical classroom discourse, practice, and professional identity construction. *Journal of Business and Technical Communication, 14*, 5–37. doi: 10.1177/10506519001400101

Dannels, D. P. (2001). Time to speak up: A theoretical framework of situated pedagogy and practice for communication across the curriculum. *Communication Education, 50*, 144–58. doi: 10.1080/03634520109379240

Dannels, D. P. (2002). Communication across the curriculum and in the disciplines: Speaking in engineering. *Communication Education, 51*, 254–68. doi: 10.1080/03634520216513

Dannels, D.P. (2003). Teaching and learning design presentations in engineering: Contradictions between academic and workplace activity systems. *Journal of Business and Technical Communication, 17*, 139–69. doi: 10.1177/1050651902250946

Dannels, D. P. (2005). Performing tribal rituals: A genre analysis of "crits" in design studios. *Communication Education, 54*, 136–60. doi:10.1080/03634520500213165

Dannels, D. P. (2010). Communication across the curriculum problematics and possibilities: Standing at the forefront of educational reform. In D. L. Fassett & J. T. Warren (Eds.), *The Sage handbook of communication instruction* (pp. 55–79). Thousand Oaks, CA.: Sage.

Dannels, D. P., Anson, C. M., Bullard, L., & Peretti, S. (2003). Challenges in learning communication skills in engineering. *Communication Education, 52*, 50–56. doi: 10.1080/03634520302454

Dannels, D. P., Gaffney, A., & Martin, K. (2008). Beyond content, deeper than delivery: What critique feedback reveals about communication expectations in design education. *International Journal for the Scholarship of Teaching and Learning, 2*. Retrieved from http://academics.georgiasouthern.edu/ijsotl/v2n2/articles/PDFs/Article_Dannels_et_al.pdf

Dannels, D. P., & Norris Martin, K. (2008). Critiquing critiques: A genre analysis of feedback across novice to expert design studios. *Journal of Business and Technical Communication, 22*, 135–59. doi: 10.1177/1050651907311923

Darling, A. L., & Dannels, D. P. (2003). Practicing engineers talk about the importance of talk: A report on the role of oral communication in the workplace. *Communication Education, 52*, 1–16. doi: 10.1080/03634520302457

Donahue, P. (2002). Strange resistance. *The WAC Journal, 13*, 31–41. Retrieved from wac.colostate.edu/journal/vol13/donahue.pdf

Hall, E. & Hughes, B. (2011). Preparing faculty, professionalizing fellows: Keys to success with undergraduate writing fellows in WAC. *The WAC Journal, 22,* 21–40. Retrieved from: wac.colostate.edu/journal/vo122/hall.pdf

Hansen, K. & Adams, J. (2010). Teaching writing in the social sciences: A comparison and critique of three models. *Across the disciplines, 7.* Retrieved from wac.colostate.edu/atd/articles/Hansen_adams2010.cfm

Herrington, A. J. (1985). Writing in academic settings: A study of the contexts or writing in two college chemical engineering courses. *Research in the Teaching of English, 19,* 331–59.

Huba, M. E. & Freed, J. E. (2000). *Learner-centered assessment on college campuses: Shifting the focus from teaching to learning.* Boston, MA: Allyn & Bacon.

Huber, M. T., & Morreale, S. P. (Eds.). (2002). *Disciplinary styles in the scholarship of teaching and learning: Exploring common ground.* Washington, DC: American Association of Higher Education.

Jablonski, J. (2006). *Academic writing consulting and WAC: methods and models for guiding cross-curricular literacy work.* Cresskill, NJ: Hampton Press.

Knowles, M. (1980). *The modern practice of adult education.* New York, NY: Association Press.

Mehrabian, A. (1981). *Silent messages: Implicit communication of emotions and attitudes* (2nd ed.). Belmont, CA: Wadsworth.

Melzer, D. (2014). The connected curriculum: Designing a vertical transfer writing curriculum. *The WAC Journal, 25,* 78–91. Retrieved from wac.colostate.edu/journal/vo125/melzer.pdf

Mezirow, J. (2000). Learning to think like an adult: Core concepts of transformation theory. In J. Mezirow & Associates (Eds.), *Learning as transformation: critical perspectives on a theory in progress* (pp. 3–33). San Francisco, CA: Jossey-Bass.

Mezirow, J. (2003). Transformative learning as discourse. *Journal of Transformative Education, 1,* 58–63. Doi: 10.1177/1541344603252172

Paretti, M. (2011). Interdisciplinarity as a lens for theorizing language/content partnerships. *Across the Disciplines* 8(3). Retrieved from http://wac.colostate.edu/atd/articles/paretti2011.cfm

Reitmeier, C. A. & Vrchota, D. A. (2009). Self-assessment of oral communication presentations in Food Science and Human Nutrition. *Journal of Food Science Education, 8,* 88–92. doi: 10.1111/j,1541-4329.2009.00080

Reitmeier, C.A., Svendsen, L.K., & Vrchota, D.A. (2004). Improving oral communication skills for students in food science courses. *Journal of Food Science Education, 3,* 15–20.

Robinson, H. & Hall, J. (2013). Connecting WID and the writing center: Tools for collaboration. *The WAC Journal, 24,* 29–7. Retrieved from wac.colostate.edu/journal/vo124/robinson.pdf

Rodrigue, T. K. (2012). The (in)visible world of teaching assistants in the disciplines: Preparing TAs to teach writing. *Across the Disciplines, 9*(1). Retrieved from http://wac.colostate.edu/atd/articles/rodrigue2012.cfm

Ronesi, L. (2011). "Striking while the iron is hot." A writing fellows program supporting lower-division courses at an American university in the UAE. *Across the Disciplines, 8*(4). Retrieved from http://wac.colostate.edu/atd/articles/ronesi2011.cfm

Rutz, C. & Grawe, N.D. (2009). Pairing WAC and quantitative reasoning through portfolio assessment and faculty development. *Across the Disciplines, 6*. Retrieved from http://wac.colostate.edu/atd/assessment/rutz_grawe.cfm

Schein, E. (1987). *Process consultation: Lessons for managers and consultants.* Reading, MA: Addison-Wesley.

Soliday, M. (2011). *Everyday genres: Writing assignments across the disciplines.* Carbondale: Southern Illinois University Press.

Stout, R. P. (2011). "It's a shame to put such wonderful thoughts in such poor language": A chemist's perspective on writing in the disciplines. *Across the Disciplines, 8*(1). Retrieved from http://wac.colostate.edu/atd/articles/stout2011/index.cfm

Tarabochia, S. (2013). Language and relationship building: Analyzing discursive spaces of interdisciplinary collaboration. *Across the Disciplines,10*(2). Retrieved from http://wac.colostate.edu/atd/articles/tarabochia2013.cfm

Taylor, K. (2000). Teaching with developmental intention. In J. Mezirow & Associates (Eds), *Learning as Transformation: Critical Perspectives on a Theory in Progress* (pp. 151–80). San Francisco, CA: Jossey-Bass.

Vrchota, D. (2011). Communication in the disciplines: Interpersonal communication in dietetics. *Communication Education, 60,* 210–30. 10.1080/03634523.2010.523475

Vrchota, D. A. (2012, November). Communicating in the disciplines: Communication about food in food science. Paper presented at the annual conference of the National Communication Association, Orlando, FL.

Vrchota, D. A. & Russell, D. R. (2013). WAC/WID meets CXC/CID: A dialogue between writing studies and communication studies. *The WAC Journal, 24,* 49–62.

Vrchota, D. A. (2015a). A view of oral communication in food science from the perspective of a communication researcher. *Journal of Food Science, 14,* 36–47. doi. 10.1111/1541-4329.12056

Vrchota, D. A. (2015b, April). Converging across the curriculum: When communication and disciplinary faculty work together. Paper presented at the annual conference of the Central States Communication Association, Madison, WI.

Walvoord, B., Hunt, L., Dowling, H., McMahon, J. (1997). *In the long run: A study of faculty in three writing-across-the-curriculum programs.* Urbana, IL: NCTE.

Winsor, D.A. (1994). Invention and writing in technical work: Representing the object. *Written Communication, 11,* 227–50.

Witt, P. L. & Wheeless, L. R. (2001). An experimental study of teachers' verbal and nonverbal immediacy and students' affective and cognitive learning. *Communication Education, 50,* 327–42.

Wolfe, J., Olson, B., & Wilder, L. (2014). Knowing what we know about writing in the disciplines: A new approach to teaching for transfer in FYC. *The WAC Journal, 25,* 42–77. Retrieved from wac.colostate.edu/journal/vo125/wolfeetal.pdf

At the Commencement of an Archive: The National Census of Writing and the State of Writing Across the Curriculum

CAITLIN CORNELL HOLMES

> As we have noted all along, there is an incessant tension here between the archive and archaeology. They will always be close the one to the other, resembling each other, hardly discernible in their co-implication, and yet radically incompatible, heterogeneous.
>
> —Jacques Derrida

In his seminal theorization of the archive, Jacques Derrida offers a deconstructive reading of Sigmund Freud in three parts: Freud the person, Freud the archive, and Freud the text.[1] Derrida maintains that these disparate yet interrelated entities complicate whatever archive a researcher may hope to analyze, reminding us that there is always something that cannot be represented in archival work: the "remainder" that is left out. Archives—and the databases that constitute them—have since remained a focal point within rhetoric and composition as an emerging and evolving field, often calling attention to what is included and excluded as we reposition our discourses about writing program administration and writing pedagogies.[2] For example, *College English*'s (1999) special volume on archival work in rhetoric and composition reinforces the extent to which the archive has been central to questions of positioning writing within higher education, specifically with regard to which texts ought to be used to define the field. As John Brereton (1999) notes in his introduction to that very collection, "we still aren't sure what should be in our archive, or how access can be broadened, or which tools we should bring to our task of exploring the past. In fact, we aren't sure exactly what we already have in our archive, or how in fact we even define the term" (p. 574). He reminds us that "our term 'archive' is hardly static" (p. 576): the resources that help document and capture rhetoric and composition practices are indeed myriad and complex.

On a more local level, institutional or programmatic histories collected through archives—such as those collected by Gretchen Flesher Moon and Patricia Donahue—can subvert what has been established at the national level in terms of scholarly trends and concerns. Traditional archives composed of historical documents at institutions long affiliated with WAC (Arizona State University and George Mason University are but two examples) have emerged as an excellent source of information about programmatic development over time. These archives are immensely useful, as Susan Wells (2002) argues in her discussion of Walter Benjamin's *The Arcades Project*. Drawing upon Derrida as well, she claims that the "final gift of the archives is the possibility of reconfiguring our disciplines" (p. 60). Wells notes that archives are defined by what we choose to include and exclude. Inclusion consequently changes the nature of what we think and observe about a field of study, expanding or limiting our evidence or dataset. In the case of WAC, I would amend her statement from "reconfiguring our disciplines" to "reconfiguring how we situate and represent our larger scholarly conversation and practices."

Archives, however, are not necessarily limited to collections of documents preserved in special collections. Rather, with the great advances made in information technology in recent decades, searchable and generative databases certainly should be considered archives in and of themselves. The power of collecting such documents and data lies in the potential to test our assumptions about the implementation of principles and practices inside and outside of composition proper. In fact, Wells maintains that archival work "help[s] us to rethink our political and institutional situation" (p. 60), as she claims that archives help scholars to hedge the desire to affirm their own positions, noting that the archive "resist[s] my own drive to demonstration, told me that I needed to do more" (p. 59).[3] In other words, when our research is limited to our own institution, or one or two comparable institutions, or even larger data from a fixed point in time, we risk confirming what we already know and assuming it is the status quo. Within WAC, then, one of the primary reasons for capturing large sets of information would thereby be to test and reconsider our own assumptions about the norms and practices at institutions other than our own—to find the outliers and remainders that may not come to light under the weight of our own "drive to demonstration."

It is appropriate that at the moment of "commencement"—as Derrida would call it—for a new archive, we remain attuned to the difficulties of actualizing a new source of data within writing across the curriculum scholarship. The National Census of Writing (formerly known as the WPA Census Project, hereafter abbreviated as "NCW") is a response to needs for perspective on both the particularities of individual programs and on larger national trends of writing program development and sustainability. Not an archive in the traditional sense, the NCW database is composed both of stable institution profiles as well as searchable data represented in tables, charts, and graphs. As the census evolves in the future, it is intended that data from the past will still be tracked against new information, making it possible to compare trends over time. This opportunity to compare against archived information is especially crucial, given that since the publication of Chris Thaiss and Tara Porter's (2010) study of WAC/WID programs, there still remains a need for what they defined as "accurate, up-to-date information on the presence and characteristics of WAC and writing-in-the-disciplines (WID) programs" (p. 534).

However, much as Thaiss and Porter discovered in their 2008 survey, even reliably determining how many WAC/WID programs exist in the US and uncovering the trends in infrastructures that they exhibit—as I will illustrate in this essay—remains difficult. Data collected about programs becomes outdated almost immediately upon publication, as institutions continue to grow and evolve beyond the information they provide. These concerns are not addressed as explicitly as one would hope in past studies. To date, all efforts to survey and report on the reach and shape of WAC/WID programs—exemplified by Art Young and Susan Huber's (1984) ADE survey, Susan MacLeod and Susan Shirley's (1987) survey, and Thaiss and Porter's (2010) aforementioned work, which are the primary examples that are focused on WAC/WID initiatives within the larger milieu of writing program surveys—have been limited by the fixity of data represented in publication, the labor-intensive nature of collecting this information from individual schools, and the continuing ambiguity around how these types of writing programs are constituted and positioned within local contexts.[4] These efforts are still immensely invaluable for gaining perspective on the persistence, spread, and trends related to WAC/WID programs in the US and Canada.

In contrast to previous efforts to collect and compare data, such as those mentioned above, the NCW offers dynamic data results through inquiry and filters that will be beneficial to future research and writing program advocacy. The NCW project began in 2013, spearheaded by Jill Gladstein (Swarthmore College) and Dara Rossman Regaignon (New York University), then by Brandon Fralix (Bloomfield College), Jennifer Wells (Florida State University), and ultimately the George Mason University WAC Program faculty, which joined the project in 2014. The first of its kind for writing program researchers, the NCW database is supported by a Mellon Foundation "Scholarly Communications" grant, which was awarded to Gladstein, Regaignon, and Fralix in 2014. The initial survey collected data from a total of 680 responding schools on sites of writing instruction and support at public and not-for-profit universities with the goal of making the data collected available to researchers and program administrators via an interactive, online database. The NCW database is a powerful tool for querying information about writing programs and initiatives of all types—sites of writing, first-year composition, writing centers, WAC/WID programs, and administrative structures, and demographics for those programs—at two- and four-year institutions with a variety of filters to move from broader questions (such as "How many WAC programs are there?") to more narrow ones (such as "How many minority-serving institutions require WI?").

The NCW thereby offers a wealth of information about writing programs across the country. As a natural part of the coding and database construction process, it both flattens and reveals some of the complexities that attend WAC/WID programmatic work, and a few of these complexities and new contributions are what this essay seeks to share. Much in the vein of Derrida's criticism of the archive, any coding schema tends to exclude outliers and variability—the tension between archaeology and the archive is inevitably present. Derrida's consideration of the archive holds true here: what programs are in actuality, how programs are represented in the raw data submitted, and how programs appear in public-facing interfaces are all separate and heterogeneous things. Given the localized, embedded, and organic nature of WAC work (as Marcia Dickson (1993) has characterized it), applying a rigid coding schema to the particularities of WAC programs was an especially fraught process. As this article will demonstrate, the data collection and cleaning process revealed a variety of tensions between national discourses about writing program administration and WAC work *vis-a-vis* localized discourses that I hope will help scholars to qualify and contextualize the data that are presented in the final NCW database.

With this in mind, I will attend to areas of inquiry of particular interest to the WAC/WID scholarly community, and—as a necessary part of discussing these areas—I will include some information that will not appear in the final database. Where previous surveys have presented their data in one stable article and therefore could include a variety of responses, the NCW database will not be able to do so to nearly the same extent.[5] This outside information has been excluded from the database in part due to the limitations of coding structures and data presentation, such as algorithmic restraints, numerical tables that cannot accommodate text answers, or respondents' selection of "other" categories in datasets that had limited space for qualitative responses. Some of these "other" answers also were flattened into new categories during the cleaning process. Also, other data were omitted from the final database in part due to the related processes of collection and cleaning that allow the database computations to operate. The primary areas of investigation that center this essay concern continuing questions in defining WAC programs, questions of institutional expertise, and questions related to administrative oversight of WAC initiatives and programs in general. These three questions represent areas in which the data were either especially difficult to code—as in the case of definitional questions about what constitutes a WAC program—or where representations of institutional structures defied easy stabilization into categories.[6] While the main thrust of this essay is to highlight the relationship between included and excluded data in order to cast into better relief some of the significant challenges of data collection and archival work, I also will close by highlighting Wells's claim about helping rethink key terminology in WAC. The preliminary data presented in this piece are limited in scope, focusing on a few key factors and opportunities for researchers as they begin to utilize the new NCW database. Any qualitative information shared in this essay will remove or redact identifying institutional information so as to protect the privacy of the respondents. Please see Appendix 1 for the full questions that constitute the WAC portion of the NCW survey.

Questions Defining WAC Programs

As Thaiss and Porter articulated in their 2010 findings, defining *WAC* and *program* remains problematic in spite of a variety of sub-questions designed to tease out consistent characteristics of local WAC initiatives. After Thaiss and Porter's survey results were published, William Condon and Carol Rutz (2012) similarly noted that "As WAC's thirty-plus-year history argues, the pedagogy and associated philosophy have become widespread, yet WAC as a phenomenon does not possess a single, identifiable structure; instead, it varies in its development and its manifestation from campus to campus" (p. 358). As WAC has become more "familiar" (Thaiss and Porter, 2010, p. 536), our representations of those manifestations have become correspondingly more diverse. This particular and embedded nature of WAC programs and initiatives then causes a variety of methodological problems in relation to data collection and determining how many programs there are within the United States, much as Gladstein and Regaignon argued in their 2012 discussion of WAC/WID initiatives at small liberal arts colleges (pp. 35–41, pp. 108–119). With the diversity of metaphors used to describe WAC programs over an almost thirty-year conversation—from Marilyn Cooper's (1986) "ecology of writing" to Bill Condon and Carol Rutz's (2012) quantum mechanics to Laura Brady's (2013) comparison of WAC and evolutionary theory—it is unsurprising that defining WAC initiatives remain a slippery thing.

The NCW's first question related to WAC programs asks, "Does your institution have a WAC program and/or writing requirement beyond the first year?" The structure of this question was designed to capture as much information as possible about writing in the major or disciplinary writing instruction but did not include the language of *initiative* or *collaboration* that other surveys have included (see Thaiss and Porter, 2010).[7] Moreover, this initial question was intended to act as a gatekeeping question for those responding to the entirety of the survey. A negative answer would prevent respondents from accessing questions on WAC/WID entirely. An affirmative answer allowed respondents to access the WAC section, which required a secondary confirmation of whether or not the institution had a WAC/WID program (see Appendix 1). However, follow-up responses allowed institutions to provide further data without the gatekeeping question preventing access. The difference between these two sections is represented in Table 1.

Subsequent questions in the WAC/WID section enumerated possible writing requirements usually affiliated with WAC/WID work, which included other lower-division, upper-division, and mid-level writing courses; theses or senior writing capstones; writing-intensive courses; assessment of program or course goals; and faculty professional development. Developed by Gladstein and Regaignon in their original 2010 survey instrument, these particular question structures were originally tied to characteristics usually associated with WAC programs or initiatives, as well as the WPA Statement of Outcomes issued by the Council of Writing Program Administrators in 2000 and most recently revised in July 2014.[8] The NCW's preliminary data regarding WAC programs and/or writing requirements beyond the first year are presented in Table 2. From this preliminary data, there is an overall increase in the number of WAC programs (proportionately speaking) from previous surveys, from approximately 43% (Thaiss and Porter, 2008) to 51% (NCW, 2013).

Table 1: Comparison between sites of writing WAC/WID and secondary affirmation in WAC/WID section of survey

	Sites of Writing	WAC/WID Section	% Difference
All Respondents (n=670)	315	341	+6%

Table 2: How many 4-year institutions have WAC/WID programs and/or writing requirement beyond the first year?

	Yes	No/NR	% with WAC
All Respondents (n=670)	341	301	51%

The data presented here are complicated by two subsets of respondents: first, respondents who either opted out after reviewing the question set independently in a follow-up email; second, those who answered in the affirmative on this initial question and then filled in subsequent "Other" options with statements that indicated there was no WAC program at all. NCW data required a clear division between "Yes" (coded as a 1) and "No" (coded as a 2). There was no ambivalence for those who might have only glimmers of such requirements embedded in various sites across the institution, those who might not identify with the initial language of *program* or *writing requirement*, or those who might have structures that do not map onto the questionnaire. For example, one respondent wrote that his writing program was in the process of developing specific writing-focused support for "WID, which includes faculty development, research, consultations, and teaching"—all of which usually correspond to national discourses about WAC/WID initiatives—but the respondent did not think that their particular initiatives fit with the questions asked in the survey: "we do not technically have a program, so none of your questions really apply." In fact, several leaders of WAC initiatives said that the survey questions simply did not apply to them, questioning either the language of *programs* or the criteria often used to define such programs. One respondent from a discipline-based writing program noted that the WAC portion of the survey did not apply to her program. A different survey respondent indicated that while her institution had many characteristics of WAC, she lacked a budget for her initiatives and therefore did not believe she had a WAC program. Indeed, in spite of their institutions having the characteristics that usually define what is seen as a WAC program or "writing requirements beyond the first year," independent conversations with respondents via email or in person indicated that they were at times hesitant to identify as "WAC," noting that the absence of financial support, a particular sort of administrative oversight, or a lack of an institutional home prevented them from continuing with the survey. Ultimately, these respondents were coded as "2," indicating that the school did not have a program or disciplinary writing requirement beyond the first year, but future researchers will have the opportunity to use the NCW's filters to correlate the relationship between those respondents who did choose to identify as having a WAC program and their self-identified characteristics of WAC. Furthermore, the opposite also represents a possible wealth of research opportunities: scholars will have access to institutions who selected "No WAC" and can begin to investigate why they made that choice.

The second body of respondents who complicated the data presented in Table 2 answered affirmatively, but then populated later text-based options stating that there was not, in fact, a WAC program at their institution. In one representative example, a respondent noted that their school had a "WAC program or writing requirement beyond the first year," required some students to complete a thesis and WI courses, assessed goals related to those courses, and offered professional development to faculty teaching WI courses. However, upon reaching the end of the WAC portion of the survey, the respondent wrote, "This is not a WAC program." Another respondent also answered affirmatively to almost every question in the WAC portion of the survey, but then wrote, "no WAC program." This particular contradiction arose 14 times in the preliminary data. Even more problematic, as will be discussed in the next section, this same institution also had a second respondent who answered that there was no WAC program/writing requirement beyond the first year at all. Clearly, the structural language of *program* not only is a difficult one for scholars to discuss—as the above scholars of WAC program organization have noted—but that discontinuities in language also remain a methodological concern as scholars continue to gather data and seek to represent WAC work in our scholarship and at our own institutions.

Questions of Institutional Expertise

With the complications that arose from issues surrounding what is and is not a WAC program or writing requirement beyond the first year, it was discovered that the number of respondents identifying WAC programs at their institution had another layer of complexity that will ultimately be unseen in the final version of the NCW database. Specifically, given the distribution of WAC programs across institutions, at times it was unclear who in fact spoke most clearly for WAC. As Gladstein and Regaignon (2012) have previously articulated, the leadership of such programs can have a variety of configurations in order to foster and support different institutional goals. Similarly, leadership of WAC programs is, as was discovered in compiling and coding the NCW data, difficult to trace when it is so often embedded in the disciplines or distributed across multiple colleges, positions, and departments. This difficulty in stabilizing raw data related to a WAC/WID initiative manifested in interesting ways: respondents from the same institution shared different information and, consequently, gave conflicting answers; respondents who did not feel capable of giving information about their programs or requirements; and those who were sure there was a WAC program but did not know who at their institution might be able to provide information. While some of these concerns were resolved in follow-up emails, their very presence in the initial data raises some important questions about who speaks for WAC/WID work when leadership of those initiatives has such variable structure and—indeed—may be housed outside of usual contact areas for writing initiatives. While these conflicts may be unsurprising to scholars of WAC program institutional structure or organizational leadership, the NCW's structure accentuates a few areas and opportunities for future research.

Tables 3, 4, and 5 highlight these peculiarities related to questions of institutional or programmatic authority. Specifically, 127 schools had multiple respondents, on which only 46 respondents deferred to a different person's expertise. At 10 institutions, both respondents from the same school believed there was someone better able to respond for their institution. Furthermore, every institution whose multiple respondents went on to provide information had conflicting answers—sometimes substantial ones—in this section of the NCW. In other words, none of the multiple respondents agreed on what the components of their WAC/WID program or writing requirements were, or they defined their terms differently—even on the same campus. Of particular note were the differences of opinion about whether the institution actually had a WAC/WID program, as 22 schools with multiple respondents disagreed in this initial category. It was not an uncommon occurrence to see one respondent claim that the site had a program and to input responses to represent the features of that program and then have another respondent from the same institution reply that no WAC/WID program existed at all. While this response percentage may initially seem insignificant, further data regarding oversight of WAC programs reveal a consistent pattern of administration by committee or dispersal of oversight for these initiatives. The language of the question "Do you feel able to answer questions about writing across the curriculum or the writing requirement beyond the first year?" offered respondents the opportunity to defer to the authority of someone else on their campus. That two (or sometimes three) respondents could bring such differing views to the same questions represents an excellent opportunity to investigate the relationship between an individual's institutional position and the perceived work that occurs in WAC/WID programs. The NCW's protocol ultimately removes these differences of opinion from the final representation of an institution's sites of writing. With that in mind, these conflicting initial responses provided here are meant to offer an opportunity for further investigation of positionality and distributed leadership models within WAC administration.

Table 3: Number of schools with multiple respondents*

	Schools With Multiple Respondents	%	# of Respondents Who Deferred	% (n=127)
Total Number of Schools (n=670)	127	19%	46	36%

Table 4: Number of institutions disagreeing on presence of WAC program*

	# Disagreeing on WAC/WID Program	% Disagreeing on WAC/WID Program
Schools with Multiple Respondents (n=127)	22	17%

Table 5: Preliminary conflicting information*

	# of Multiple Respondents Completing All WAC Sections	% (n=127)	# of Multiple Respondents with Disagreements	% (n=100)
Schools with Multiple Respondents (n=127)	100	79%	99	99%

*NB: These data are composed of the multiple respondents who entered data for the WAC section of the census. There were even more multiple respondents for the entirety of the dataset across all sites of writing. All institutions with multiple respondents who had a respondent that did not provide data were excluded.

Complicating those institutions with multiple entries, the NCW also gave respondents the opportunity to opt out of providing information about their WAC initiatives depending on their level of ability to answer. The specific language of the question gave respondents a sense of the contents of the survey in order to help them self-assess their knowledge of their programs prior to proceeding:

> Do you feel able to answer questions about writing across the curriculum or the writing requirement beyond the first year? You will be asked questions about different requirements including details about writing-intensive

courses. You will also be asked about goals and assessment, faculty development, and the administration of these requirements including details on the job responsibilities of the different people who administer the program.

This question was meant for the project team to follow up with respondents or new contacts, and it is not included in the final, searchable database. Table 6 represents those respondents who indicated that there is a WAC program or writing requirement beyond the first year at their institution but did not feel they had the necessary expertise to share information about the program. At this early point in the survey, respondents who selected that they were not comfortable giving information were given the option to provide contact information for another person at the institution who might be better able to relate such information. With 32% of initial respondents indicating that they did not feel comfortable sharing information about their WAC/WID programs, it was surprising to see the comparatively low level of referrals to other colleagues at institutions. Indeed, in 13% of cases, the respondent confirmed that no other contact existed at all—the respondent was the only person who could talk about writing programs, but that ability did not extend to WAC.

Table 7 further underscores this concern, as 56% of respondents simply left the information blank. Follow-up inquiries yielded few responses, but those who responded to emails shared anecdotes about concerns at their institutions. One person characterized his institution's WAC course as "dysfunctional," stating that, "We have the requirement that every student take a discipline-based WAC course, but there is no WAC director. In fact, there has not been a WAC director since the late 1980's, and there are no plans for hiring one. . . . What's worse is that in many cases I don't even have someone I can ask for information from," as the program was "rudderless." The implicit disciplinary work that occurs in WAC initiatives seems, then, to obscure who in fact can and ought to speak for the program, as well as some of the methodologies that we might use to gather information about programs both locally and nationwide. Ultimately, respondents who provided no information in the initial survey or in response to follow-up emails will have their programs listed as "data unavailable." As it becomes possible for more schools to participate in the NCW in several years, there will be a fuller picture of the many representatives of writing programs and what perspectives they might bring as a part of their particular positions in their institutions.

Table 6: Respondent capability and referral ability*

	Total with WAC Programs (n=341)	%
Not Capable of Responding	111	33%

*NB: The number not capable of responding was taken out of the original, preliminary data.

Table 7: Respondent referral ability

	Total Not Capable of Responding (n=111)	%
Provided WAC Contact	19	17%
Unsure of WAC Contact	12	11%
No Other Contact Exists	14	13%
No Information Provided	62	56%

Questions of Program Administrative Structures

As previously discussed, there are a variety of understandings about the nature of WAC work being conducted at home institutions, which supports representations of WAC administration as being "diffused" or "democratized," even beyond the liberal arts college configurations that Gladstein and Regaignon (2012) have described (p. 61). Perhaps this trend can be attributed to the tendency of WAC programs to be absorbed into other institutional structures, such as composition programs or assessment initiatives.[9] Table 8 provides some suggestive information along these lines, as 40% of preliminary respondents with WAC programs answered "Who has primary oversight for the WAC Program?" with "Other" (out of the possible answers of WAC director, director of first-year writing, chair of the English department, writing center director, chief academic officer, registrar, associate dean or provost, faculty committee, no one, and other), thereby indicating that the single categories provided were insufficient to describe the complexities of their administrative structures. While new data columns were created to account for repeating answers, an overwhelming number of respondents took time to explain the differences between the explicit structures that had oversight by an administrator and the implicit structures that had more or less supervision by particular committees, departments, faculty, or administrators throughout the institution.

A promising trend that emerged from these qualitative responses is the collaboration that takes place as a part of these negotiated spaces, as well as the staying power that is produced by WAC initiatives even when programs may be losing momentum or are now defunct. With regard to the former, many respondents wrote that there were shared responsibilities with faculty across the institution or with organizational allies, such as those identified in the WAC Statement of Principles and Practices (2014). Where one selection of program administration was insufficient to describe the particularities of their institution, the "Other" section was utilized to identify multiple sites of administration for WAC initiatives. One respondent noted that—in addition to the WI approvals process being controlled by a cross-disciplinary university committee—program administration was "[a]nother shared responsibility, this time between the Writing Center Director and the Associate Vice Provost for Undergraduate Education (who currently serves as Director of [writing in the major])." These multiple sites of writing expertise consequently confound the extent to which any individual survey respondent could accurately represent the full scope of disciplinary writing at his or her institution. Interestingly, the description related above was not in fact submitted by the writing center director, who might have a different perspective on who bears the weight of administrative duties or—indeed—have questions about what constitutes "administration" or "oversight" in practice.

With regard to WAC's persistence, respondents who indicated that they no longer have formal programs elaborated upon the remaining cultures of writing that operate at their institutions. One respondent who selected "Other" in response to questions about program oversight wrote, "The WAC program is defunct, but still has faculty who participated in it who use its guidance." At that institution, the culture of writing created by WAC long outlasted the program's formal existence or single administrative structure. Another respondent noted that in spite of their WAC program not being an "explicit one," particular disciplinary programs had administrators who directed writing-related programs in the majors but were not generally considered experts on writing. Instead, the writing program director consulted with these disciplinary administrators to support the "implicit" writing in the disciplines practices occurring within the major. These areas of implicit "oversight" represent an interesting opportunity for further research regarding the sustainability and longevity of WAC principles at institutions where funding for such initiatives is withdrawn.

Table 8: Primary oversight of WAC program, preliminary responses*

	"Other"	%	Collaborative Description	% (n=140)
Total With WAC/WID (n=341)	140	41%	26	19%

*NB: The number of "Other" responses was taken out of the original, preliminary data. These data have since been reallocated into other, newly created categories.

Conclusion

WAC/WID programs, it has long been noted, are particularly responsive to local contexts; a tool that casts the broadest net possible may not capture all elements of interest to all researchers. The data made available by the NCW database will provide many more opportunities to its users, as correlations amongst particular sets of information—such as institution size, location, population, curriculum, and practices—confirm and confound beliefs that scholars of WAC may hold. Basic information about trends in programs nationally that are usually solicited via listservs or emerge from studies comparing select institutions will now be readily available to scholars, but, as I have tried to illustrate in this essay, it is not without need for qualification. Our struggles to gather this information in previous surveys and research are consequently not solely stemming from methodological issues rooted in the questions we are asking, but also in the unique institutional structures that make up writing across the curriculum and writing in the disciplines.

Even as some nuance is lost by the inevitable process of inclusion by study designers and other understandings obscured by respondents' interactions with the survey, much is gained in efforts to archive and present broad national data about writing programs. As Jeff Rice (2011) argued in his Latourian reading of assessment practices, this is why we benefit from following the traces and actors that compose WAC networks: in part to confirm our hunches with data-driven practices but also to resist the assumption that our national discourses circulating in publication and at our conferences apply to all of the practices that are manifesting across the country (pp. 31–32). The strength of the NCW is its power to reveal the great similarity and great variety of structures and practices—the accounts that "resist [our] own drive to demonstration" (Wells 2002, p. 59) about what we think is the norm and those that call into question the "topos that are already there" (Rice 2011, p. 32). It seems likely that the NCW survey mechanism will continue to inform its participants as much as it provides data for the field—one respondent noted in the assessment section that while his institution did not assess WI, the survey had made him think about the different types of assessment available to his program in the future. This circularity—"the survey helped me think about X, so when I fill it out next time it will be X"—represents another fascinating area of inquiry. We benefit, then, by being open to the new and unique configuration that an archive can produce knowledge.

The NCW has the potential to challenge assumptions, as well. For example, to what extent does the process of completing national surveys shape how respondents think about the formulation of their own local programs? Digital humanists such as Lev Manovitch (2012) have long noted that participants in public-facing data sources often self- "curate" to project particular images of themselves or the organizations that they represent (p. 466)—will this tendency arise as respondents consider how to represent their institutions in the best light or the most honest one? As we aim to "see the whole," as Michel Foucault (1972) put it so aptly (p. 126), what voices and discourses are being excluded by the nature of our question structures and survey logic? Such accounts and topoi are the richness that the NCW offers to the field, and the complexities represented in the datasets it will represent are much more than this essay can hope to identify or even gesture toward.

The initial examples presented here are meant to qualify some of the aggregated information presented in the census from the perspective of a researcher who had the opportunity to work with the raw data. With this in mind, the possible research areas that the NCW database will be able to further pursue are myriad. For example, what is the relationship between institution size and the preponderance of WAC programs or initiatives? What sorts of institutions conduct assessment of their WI courses? What forms of assessment get support from institutional assessment in comparison to WPA-run assessment? Is professional development something practiced widely amongst small liberal arts colleges or larger research institutions? Are faculty compensated for their time doing professional development and in what ways? How do these various categories of curricular and institutional description correlate with various filters in place? These along with many other questions can serve as foundations for scholars and administrators both to advocate for their programs at their own institutional levels and begin developing more data-driven research projects.

Perhaps the most troubling concern that the NCW raises for scholars of WAC/WID is its confirmation of continuing issues related to even defining our terms. In 2010, Thaiss and Porter sought "to define just what, to our respondents, is this 'WAC' about which we are so concerned" (p. 562). It appears that we are still in the process of defining some of these key terms. That *program* remains a controversial word even after thirty years of scholarship further underscores the importance of the NCW's work. If we are still not that far removed from what most practitioners intuitively understand, then there is an occasion for further inquiry as to why these discourses have stagnated. We seem to circle around the same terminology, describing program features with everything from figures (metaphors and similes) to comparison by negation ("we are not that" or "we do not have X"). Why is the language about WAC work so polarizing on a local and institutional level? What can we learn about our institutional structures and practices through the instability of these terms? What is at stake in developing a more stable set of definitions, and is such an endeavor in the best interest of WAC initiatives? As the NCW database begins to illustrate the unfolding of WAC initiatives across the country over time, I hope that it will provide a richer picture of how disciplinary writing "terms" itself at particular locations, while also giving scholars a stronger sense of national trends for those who identify or dis-identify with such vocabulary.

Like Thaiss and Porter, I end my discussion of some of the tensions that this data collection process has revealed with a call for further research using the NCW database. It is my hope that this essay has offered some thoughts and information that might provide opportunities and encouragement for WAC scholars, as the NCW project presents ample opportunity for others to begin asking and answering questions that they may not have had the resources or support structures to investigate independently. I look forward to seeing how the NCW database will be of use to those who will take up the challenges its data represent to offer further understandings of the changing WAC/WID landscape.

Notes

1. I would like to thank the National Census of Writing team, Jill Gladstein and Brandon Fralix, for their long-term support of my work on this project and their willingness to allow me to participate in this momentous project. I would also like to thank Michelle LaFrance for her guidance of my research throughout the writing process. To the reviewers and editor of this article, thank you for your kind and supportive feedback.

2. See Marlene Manoff's 2004 work, *Theories of the Archive from Across the Disciplines*, for a fully elaborated discussion of defining *archive* in cross-disciplinary and digital contexts.

3. Wells cites other notable discussions of the archive, including Susan Miller's *Assuming the Positions*, Robert Connors' *Composition-Rhetoric*, and Jacqueline Royster's *Traces of a Stream*, as a part of the importance of archival work within rhetoric and composition studies.

4. There have been other notable examples of such surveys, including C.W. Griffin's (1985) survey of WAC programs, Barbara Stout and Joyce Magnotto's (1987) survey of community college WAC programs, Leslie Roberts's (2008) study of community and two-year college WAC and writing center programs.

5. See, for example, Thaiss & Porter's (2010) inclusion of comments and explanations throughout their work.

6. See Krista Kennedy and Seth Long (2015) for a detailed breakdown of the complexities of data work in "The Trees in the Forest: Extracting, Coding, and visualizing Subjective Data in Authorship Studies."

7. The National Census of Writing website has a full glossary to assist researchers and future respondents when it is available for update in 2017.

8. The CWPA Statement was subsequently reworked into the WAC Statement on Principles and Practices and approved in February, 2014.

9. Carol Rutz describes her fears of this precise situation in an interview with Laura Brady (2013). Rutz says, "my teaching could be absorbed by a department, my portfolio work could be absorbed by the assessment office, and my faculty development work could be absorbed by the Center for Teaching and Learning. While the College could get it all covered that way, there would be no leadership model, and—as Ed White has said—having no leadership is risky. There would be no one to pay attention, to do the tending" (p. 15).

References

Anson, C. M. (2006). Assessing writing in cross-curricular programs: Determining the locus of activity. Assessing Writing, 11(2), 100–12.

Brady, L. (2013). Evolutionary metaphors for understanding WAC/WID. The WAC Journal, 23, 7–28.

Brereton, J.C. (1999). Rethinking Our Archive: A Beginning. College English, 61(5), 574–76.

Condon, W., & Rutz, C. (2012). A taxonomy of writing across the curriculum programs: Evolving to serve broader agendas. College Composition and Communication, 64(2), 357–82.

Cooper, M. (1986). The Ecology of Writing. College English, 48(4), 364–75.

Council of Writing Program Administrators. WPA Outcomes Statement for First-Year Composition (3.0), Approved July 17, 2014. Council of Writing Program Administrators. Retrieved from http://wpacouncil.org/positions/outcomes.html

Dickson, M. (1993). Directing without Power: Adventures in Constructing a Model of Feminist Writing Program Administration. In S.I. Fontaine & S. Hunter (Eds.), Writing ourselves into the story: unheard voices from composition studies, 140–53. Carbondale: Southern Illinois University Press.

Donohue, P. & Moon, G.F. (Eds.). (2007). Local Histories: Reading the Archives of Composition. PA: University of Pittsburgh Press.

Foucault, M. (1972). The Archaeology of Knowledge & The Discourse on Language. A.M. Sheridan Smith (Trans.). New York, NY: Pantheon Books.

Gladstein, J., & Regaignon, D. (2012). Writing Program Administration at Small Liberal Arts Colleges. Anderson, SC: Parlor Press.

Griffin, C. W. (1985). Programs for Writing Across the Curriculum: A Report. College Composition and Communication, 36(4), 398–403.

Holdstein, D. (2001). "Writing Across the Curriculum" and the Paradoxes of Institutional Initiatives. Pedagogy: Critical Approaches to Teaching Literature, Language, Composition, and Culture, 1(1), 37–52.

Huber, B. J., & Young, A. (1986). Report on the 1983–84 Survey of the English Sample. ADE Bulletin, 84, 40–61.

International Network of WAC Programs (2014). Statement of WAC Principles and Practices. The WAC Clearinghouse. Retrieved from http://wac.colostate.edu/principles/statement.pdf.

Kennedy, K. & Long, S. (2015). The Trees within the Forest: Extracting, Coding, and Visualizing Subjective Data in Authorship Studies. In J. Ridolfo & W. Hart-Davidson (Eds.), Rhetoric and the Digital Humanities (140–52). IL: The University of Chicago Press.

MacLeod, S. and Shirley, S. (1988). National Survey of WAC Programs. In S. McLeod (Ed.), Strengthening Programs for Writing Across the Curriculum (103–30). San Francisco, CA: Jossey-Bass, Inc.

Manoff, M. (2004) Theories of the Archive form Across the Disciplines. Libraries and the Academy, 4 (1), 9–25.

Rice, J. (2011). Networked Assessment. Computers and Composition, 28(1), 28–39.

Roberts, L. (2008). An analysis for the national TYCA research initiative survey section IV: Writing across the curriculum and writing centers in two-year college English programs. Teaching English in the Two-Year College, 36(2), 138–52.

Stout, B.R., & Magnotto, J.N. (1987). Writing Across the Curriculum at Community Colleges. In S. McLeod (Ed.), Strengthening Programs for Writing Across the Curriculum (21–30). San Francisco, CA: Jossey-Bass, Inc.

Thaiss, C., & Porter, T. (2010). The State of WAC/WID in 2010: Methods and Results of the U.S. Survey of the International WAC/WID Mapping Project. College Composition and Communication, 61(3), 534–70.

Wells, S. (2002). Claiming the Archive for Rhetoric and Composition. In G. Olson (Ed.), Rhetoric and Composition as Intellectual Work (55–64). Carbondale: Southern Illinois University Press.

White, E. (1990). The damage of innovations set adrift. The American Association for Higher Education, 43(3), 3–5.

Appendix 1: National Census of Writing Survey Questions (Survey Protocol Authors: Jill Gladstein and Dara Rossman Regaignon

Questions about Components of the Writing Program

1. Does your institution have a writing program?
2. What does the program consist of: Check all that apply.
    - first-year writing
    - writing across the curriculum
    - writing in the disciplines
    - undergraduate writing major
    - undergraduate writing minor
    - graduate program in writing/rhetoric
    - writing center
    - writing fellows
    - basic writing
    - other _____
    - hybrid WAC/WID program

Specific Questions for WAC and Writing Beyond the First Year

General Description

1. Does your institution require all students take lower-division writing courses taught by English or Writing for students in other departments? Does not include the first-year writing requirement.
2. Does your institution require all students take upper-division writing courses taught by English or Writing for students in other departments?
3. Does your institution require all students take a mid-level writing course(s)?
4. How would you describe the mid-level course? Check all that apply.
   - The course is focused on research writing.
   - The course is classified as writing in the major.
   - The course is similar to a writing-intensive course.
   - Each department determines which course fits this requirement.
   - Writing goals are embedded into a mid-level foundations course.
   - Other_____
5. Does your institution require all students complete a senior thesis or other writing-intensive capstone experience?
   - Yes
   - No
6. Is the senior thesis an explicit part of the college writing requirement?
   - Yes
   - No
7. Does the institution require some students to complete a senior thesis or other writing-intensive capstone experience? Check all that apply.
   - It varies by department.
   - Honors students are required to complete a thesis or other writing-intensive capstone experience.
   - No student is required to complete a senior thesis or writing-intensive capstone experience.
   - Individual students can choose to complete a senior thesis or other writing-intensive capstone experience.
   - Other _____

Writing-Intensive Courses

Do you use this form of assessment in your WAC program?	Who is responsible for administering this assessment?				Who participates in this assessment?				Explain.
Yes (1)	WPA (1)	writing program faculty (2)	faculty across the institution (3)	other (4)	WPA (1)	writing program faculty (2)	faculty across the institution (3)	other (4)	Comments (1)
paper portfolio (1)									
electronic portfolio (2)									
random sample of student writing (3)									
writing exam (4)									
professor evaluation (5)									
no assessment (6)									
other (7)									

1. Does your institution require all students take writing-intensive (WI or W) courses taught by departments other than English or Writing? These courses may be called writing attentive, writing embedded, etc.

2. How long has the WI requirement been in existence?
   - ☐ less than a year
   - ☐ 1–3 years
   - ☐ 3–5 years
   - ☐ 5–10 years
   - ☐ 10–15 years
   - ☐ 15+ years

3. How many WI courses are required beyond the first-year requirement?
   - ☐ 0
   - ☐ 1
   - ☐ 2
   - ☐ 3
   - ☐ 4
   - ☐ 5
   - ☐ 6
   - ☐ 7+

4. When do WI courses need to be completed?
   - ☐ by graduation
   - ☐ by the end of freshman year

- ☐ by the end of sophomore year
- ☐ by the end of junior year
- ☐ it depends _____

5. Are there explicit goals for the WI courses?
6. Are they publicly available? Please post link here.
7. Have the goals been influenced by the WPA Outcomes Statement?
8. How are these goals assessed? Check all that apply. If the box below is bigger than your screen, scroll right to find a comments box to discuss the nuances of your program in regards to the different assessment methods. The category other allows you to share a method that was not listed.
9. What are the criteria for a WI course? Check all that apply.
    - ☐ Certain number of pages of writing. (Feel free to include the specific number.) _____
    - ☐ Revision
    - ☐ Time discussing writing in class
    - ☐ Other_____
10. If the criteria are publicly available, please post url here.
11. Who certifies that a course meets the WI designation? Check all that apply.
    - ☐ curriculum committee
    - ☐ writing committee
    - ☐ other faculty committee
    - ☐ registrar
    - ☐ chief academic officer (provost, dean, etc.)
    - ☐ WPA
    - ☐ no one
    - ☐ other _____
12. Is there an incentive offered for faculty to teach a WI course?
    - ☐ Yes
    - ☐ No
13. Which incentives are offered? Check all that apply.
    - ☐ use of writing fellows
    - ☐ stipend
    - ☐ course release
    - ☐ smaller class size
    - ☐ credit toward tenure and promotion
    - ☐ other_____

Faculty Development for WAC

1. Is there professional or faculty development available for those teaching in the WAC program?
2. What form does that faculty development take? Check all that apply.
    - ☐ faculty seminar
    - ☐ required faculty workshops
    - ☐ optional faculty workshops
    - ☐ individual meetings with faculty members
    - ☐ collaborative research projects
    - ☐ conferences off-campus
    - ☐ on-campus speakers
    - ☐ other_____
3. If faculty are required to attend a seminar or workshop how are they compensated? Check all that apply.
    - ☐ They do not receive compensation.
    - ☐ They receive food at the event.
    - ☐ They receive a stipend.
    - ☐ They receive a grant to be used on course materials.
    - ☐ other_____

Administration of WAC

1. Who has primary responsibility for administering the WAC Program?
    - ☐ WAC director
    - ☐ director of first-year writing
    - ☐ chair of the English department
    - ☐ writing center director
    - ☐ chief academic officer
    - ☐ registrar
    - ☐ associate dean or provost
    - ☐ faculty committee
    - ☐ no one
    - ☐ other_____
2. How is the WAC director position classified?
    - ☐ tenure-line faculty
    - ☐ non-tenure line faculty (full-time)
    - ☐ non-tenure line faculty (part-time)
    - ☐ both faculty and staff (full-time)
    - ☐ both faculty and staff (part-time)

- ☐ staff only (full-time)
- ☐ staff only (part time)

3. Where does the tenure line reside?
   - ☐ English
   - ☐ Rhetoric/Composition or Writing Studies
   - ☐ Department other than English or Writing Studies_____

4. Who does the WAC director report to? (check all that apply.)
   - ☐ chair of the department
   - ☐ director of first-year writing
   - ☐ writing center director
   - ☐ chief academic officer (dean, provost, etc.)
   - ☐ associate dean or provost. (Please include title.) _____
   - ☐ dean of students
   - ☐ faculty committee
   - ☐ registrar
   - ☐ other_____

5. Was the director hired for this position?

6. How did he/she assume these responsibilities?
   - ☐ position rotates amongst faculty in the department
   - ☐ position rotates amongst all faculty
   - ☐ previous director retired or left the position
   - ☐ the director started the program after being hired
   - ☐ responsibilities are embedded in the responsibilities of the chair of the department
   - ☐ other_____

7. What is the full-time teaching load at your institution for all full-time faculty?
   - ☐ 2–2
   - ☐ 2–1–2
   - ☐ 2–2–2
   - ☐ 2–3 or 3–2
   - ☐ 3–3
   - ☐ 3–1–2
   - ☐ 3–1–3
   - ☐ 3–4 or 4–3
   - ☐ 4–4
   - ☐ 4–5 or 5–4
   - ☐ 5–5
   - ☐ 6–6
   - ☐ other_____

8. How many courses does the WAC director teach a year?
    - ☐ 0–0
    - ☐ 0–1
    - ☐ 1–1
    - ☐ 1–2 or 2–1
    - ☐ 2–2
    - ☐ 2-1-2
    - ☐ 2-2-2
    - ☐ 2–3 or 3–2
    - ☐ 3–3
    - ☐ 3-1-2
    - ☐ 3-1-3
    - ☐ 3–4 or 4–3
    - ☐ 4–4
    - ☐ 4–5 or 5–4
    - ☐ 5–5
    - ☐ 6–6
    - ☐ other _____

9. Which of the following are the job responsibilities of the WAC director?
    - ☐ teach courses in the first-year writing program
    - ☐ teach courses in the writing program/department (not FYW)
    - ☐ teaching courses outside the writing program/department
    - ☐ assess all aspects of the writing program
    - ☐ assess the development of student writing on campus
    - ☐ conduct faculty development with faculty across the disciplines
    - ☐ conduct TA training
    - ☐ consult with individual faculty across the disciplines
    - ☐ consult with departments across the disciplines
    - ☐ supervise professional staff (writing center director, asst. director, admin asst.)
    - ☐ supervise tutors (professional and/or peer)
    - ☐ hire professional staff
    - ☐ hire tutors
    - ☐ schedule writing courses
    - ☐ schedule writing center
    - ☐ place students into writing courses
    - ☐ facilitate placement exam
    - ☐ oversee curriculum development
    - ☐ train professional staff

- ☐ train peer/professional tutors
- ☐ advertise program
- ☐ oversee program budget
- ☐ tutor students
- ☐ plan events
- ☐ serve on university committees
- ☐ maintain program website
- ☐ serve as an academic advisor
- ☐ offer student workshops
- ☐ oversee exemption and/or transfer credit
- ☐ other _____

10. Does the WAC program have administrative assistants? How many? Mark zero is no support available.
    - ☐ _____ full-time administrative assistant who only works with the writing program/department
    - ☐ _____ full-time administrative assistant who splits time with another department
    - ☐ _____ part-time administrative assistant
    - ☐ _____ intern
    - ☐ _____ graduate students
    - ☐ _____ work-study students
    - ☐ _____ other

11. How many graduate students, staff members or faculty members in addition to the WAC director, have administrative responsibilities for the WAC Program or writing requirements beyond the first year?
    - ☐ 0
    - ☐ 1
    - ☐ 2
    - ☐ 3
    - ☐ 4
    - ☐ 5

For the number the survey will loop through questions 2–9.

Do You Believe in Good Academic Writing?

MARY HEDENGREN

Sword, Helen. *Stylish Academic Writing*. Cambridge MA: Harvard UP, 2012. ($21.95; 219 pp. hardback)

Helen Sword's *Stylish Academic Writing* is committed to a radical proposition: there is such a thing as universally good academic writing. Since the 1990s, the idea of general "good academic writing" has been like a unicorn, elusive because non-existent.

Can (or Should?) Good Academic Writing Exist?

We didn't doubt the existence of enjoyable scholarly articles or academic writers who are consistently able to simultaneously delight and inform. We still found writing that was good in its own context. It's just that we thought it hopelessly naïve to identify and demand a stable, universal style of writing that could apply to any discipline, any purpose, any audience. Led by Susan Peck MacDonald's *Professional Academic Writing*—which proclaims "Blanket condemnations of passive verbs, for instance, or prescriptions for vividly concrete verbs are largely ineffectual because they take no account of either the historical situatedness or the complex of knowledge-making goals and rhetorical situations represented in different kinds of academic writing" (17)—we moved style into the world of specific disciplines and dismissed with a world-weary sigh the departmental traditionalists who believed that the writing principles learned in first-year composition could be blithely applied to any class or project. Catalyzed by research in transfer, genre theory and disciplinary writing, writing across the curriculum was morphing into writing in the disciplines.

We were abandoning the entire enterprise of making certain that students and colleagues had a copy of Strunk and White inscribed in the fleshy tablets of their hearts. We knew better, now, to trust that each discipline knew better than we what good writing looked like, and scholars from Ken Hyland on down turned their attention to describing what disciplinary writing looked like in a variety of discrete fields and genres.

Good academic writing was dead.

Except it never was. Helen Sword's accessible academic-writing handbook, aimed at practicing academics, reminds us that for all of our disciplinary boundaries, we continue to admire those academic writers who "express complex ideas clearly and precisely; produce elegant, carefully crafted sentences; . . . provide their readers with aesthetic and intellectual pleasure and write with originality, imagination and creative flair" (7–8).

These virtues (reminiscent as they are of Strunk and White or Zinsser's *On Writing Well*) are backed by Sword's corpus, which is as robust as any other discourse analyst's, and her interviews with more than seventy informants across the disciplinary spectrum. *Stylish Academic Writing* provides many of the helpful hints, sample texts and end-of-chapter exercises that stand-alone handbooks have long provided, but in the context of natural language analysis, published by Sword elsewhere as academic articles. Her academic chops are present throughout the text, but she leads with an extensive discussion of her terms, methods and limitations.

Stylish Academic Writing starts with a nearly thirty-page methods section. There is an element, which Sword does not deny, of "curiosity, expertise, ignorance and serendipity" (15) in her choice of which disciplines she investigates: medicine, evolutionary biology, computer science, higher education, psychology, anthropology, law, philosophy, history and literary studies (9). This very human research practice may disincline some readers to accept her conclusions, but Sword is at least up-front about her methods. Together with an appendix and hearty bibliography, this extensive discussion of her methods seeks to root her writing suggestions in language research practices that might sound familiar to devotees of Swales and Hyland and also may provide Sword with some credence for readers in the social sciences. Books on "good style" are plentiful, but rarely are they grounded in anything other than the author's own preference and confidence.

The bulk of the book isolates what Sword cheekily titles *Elements of Stylishness:* eleven chapters on topics as diverse as writing "Tempting Titles" to avoiding "Jargonitis." None of the suggestions are, for writing administrators, particularly revolutionary, but as a resource for writing in the disciplines, the frequent examples from computer science and exercises that encourage scientists to consider the pros and cons of an IMRD structure (135) make this style handbook immediately grounded in academic writing. Every chapter argues that good writing can exist in every discipline and that good writing in each discipline will have some similar characteristics.

Sword doesn't minimize the differences between academic writing in the disciplines *as they are,* but in "encourg[ing] readers to look beyond their disciplinary barricades" (16), she highlights how artificial and how permeable those barricades are. This is crucial to her project and ours for three reasons.

First, our insistence on absolute disciplinary autonomy has been grounded in the assumption that expert discourse communities can speak among themselves however they damn-well please without the English department's input—thank you very much. Traditionally, English departments took control of teaching writing to undergraduates and set the rules for "good academic writing" throughout the university and the gains we have made in challenging this traditional—and still perniciously prevalent—view are not to be dismissed lightly. What is true in a pedagogical setting is certainly true within expert discourse communities, and I will defend to the day I die the right for discourse communities to set and shape their own generic expectations.

However, recent politics from the international level down to the department have only highlighted the need for experts to learn how to speak not only to each other but also to others. As Sword puts it, while there "will always be a place" for esoteric genres and styles, we still "do need to interact with wider audiences at least occasionally" (10). If style is keeping us from being understood when we talk to administrators, to reporters, and to the parents of our children's friends, then we need to reconsider the disciplinary virtues of generalist writing. Generalist, sometimes journalistic, writing in first-year composition has become anathema in some circles of WID scholarship, as we insisted that specialists aren't generalists. But if generalists are just people who speak to a general public, then maybe it's time to reintroduce specialists back to the public.

Second, the descriptions that we have given to disciplinary writing are sometimes too static and monolithic. We tend to speak about "the way" that biologists or engineers or psychologists write as if disciplines weren't subject to the same changes that everything is. In describing disciplinary writing in static ways, we have sometimes committed the same sins of essentialization that MacDonald justly condemns, except instead of saying "never use passive voice," we have said "scientists use the passive voice." Indeed, Sword's corpus challenges some of our received knowledge of disciplinary style, finding that philosophers eschew nominalizations, biologists embrace first-person pronouns and IMRD doesn't seem to be requisite in *every* published science article (18–19). Even when her research supports what we tell ourselves about a discipline, she finds exceptions. The existence of these exceptions among successfully-published articles implies that disciplinary writing is not rigid: being readable and engaging will not necessarily preclude your work from publication.

Third, we may have embraced a "you do you" attitude towards disciplinary academic writing since the rise of WID, but Sword isn't content to stay in a descriptive vein. If disciplinary writing is not static, if it can change, then there's no particular reason that it can't change towards a public, generalist, journalistic style. "We all have the power to change the contours" of disciplinary writing, Sword says, "*if we choose to*" (10 emphasis in original). Indeed if "convention is not a compulsion; a trend is not a law" (22), then perhaps there is something that disciplinary writers can be taught about good academic writing.

If Good Academic Writing Exists, What Does It Look Like? How Do We Write It?

Each chapter in the *Elements of Stylishness* section explores a different "element" ranging from abstracts and overall organization to the niceties of concrete language. Even citation formats get their own style chapter. But within this diverse range of topics, Sword includes similar patterns, all drawn from genre and literacy studies. She acculturates us to "good academic writing" slowly and by building on our own experience.

Each chapter begins with some data-driven generalizations drawn out from her own research. For instance, when discussing voice, Sword backs her defense of first-person pronouns with the finding that "of the sixty-six peer-reviewed journals in my cross-disciplinary study, I found only one—a prominent history journal—that apparently forbids personal pronouns" (36). Similarly, the long-taught lore of "party in the front: business in the back" colon-divided titles falls on its face when Sword notes that only twenty-two percent of titles in her sample were categorized as both engaging and informative—even though forty-eight percent contained colons and those groups did not necessarily correlate (68). She buttresses her somewhat counterintuitive stance on disciplinary writing style with the type of research that WID scholars find convincing. It's not just that she uses the raw aggregate, though.

Each chapter also contains at least one "Spotlight on Style" profile, where Sword gives models for emulation and commentary. Some of the models are well-known writer-scholars, like Oliver Sacks and Stephen Greenblatt, but Sword also includes lesser-known writers like Mike Crang and Shanthi Ameratunga because public health researchers and geographers, as we know, are also writers. The samples are long enough to put the illustrated principle in context without being cumbersome, and neither is Sword unfailingly hortatory: "Despite a plethora of *be* verbs and some sloppy locutions that demonstrated the pitfalls of abstractions," she starts out one sentence that will end with a paean to the model's overall structure (124). Providing both quantitative data and a more qualitative analysis creates a data-backed starting point before moving into her prescriptive suggestions.

The chapters are full of examples and counter-examples and—fittingly—some very engaging academic prose, but, like a good educator in disciplinary writing, Sword doesn't finish a chapter without suggesting introspective, exploratory, low-risk homework. One exercise suggests collecting a commonplace book of anecdotes relating to your field (109), while another recommends analyzing the introduction of an article you admire (85). These exercises feel as descriptive as any work John Swales might do. It's not all applied linguistics, though—there are plenty of descriptive exercises that encourage writers to identity passive verb constructions because although "a few passive phrases can provide welcome syntactical variety," too many "will add up to lifeless, agentless prose" (61).

Sword is, ultimately, writing a handbook. It's a text that can be assigned in introductory graduate-level courses and one that writing centers can keep on-hand. It's one on which deans, dissertation advisors, and others can slap a "read this" post-it note and give to whomever they see as a "struggling writer." In the course of my own practice working with graduate students across the disciplines, I find myself often referring to dog-eared sections of *Stylish Academic Writing* when someone asks about abstracts or introductions or another mystifying aspect of academic writing. I'm not embarrassed to show an economics or chemical engineering student Sword's book because she has incorporated some of the best practices of research and teaching to come out of writing in the disciplines, using a fairly robust data-set derived from practitioner informants. It's not that I believe there are easy answers to the questions of what makes good writing, but if there are going to be handbooks written about academic style, they ought to at least be research-based.

Stylish Academic Writing isn't enough on its own, of course. The students I work with deserve to see writing as multi-faceted, multi-stage and, often, multi-authored, and that has never been the strength of a single handbook. The handbook genre notoriously downplays the role of co-authors and editors, of peer-review and the continual give-and-take of editorial standards in shaping disciplinary writing. Handbooks, by their nature, are about "quick-and-easy" tips, often for self-taught writers, who are often bootstrapping in isolation. The best academic writing, the writing by the exemplary authors referenced here, happens in the context of vision and revision, of commentary and compromise. Furthermore, the conventions of disciplines, sub-disciplines and individual journals are hardly static; fresh academic writing today may be cliché tomorrow. Despite all of these caveats, Stylish Academic Writing is destined to be one of the classics of academic style handbooks for its focus on advanced academic writing (as opposed to literary or journalistic writing), for its foundation in empirical analysis (as opposed to the lore of the English department), and for its audacious project of discovering good academic writing. Perhaps Sword knows that she's suggesting the existence of unicorns. Perhaps we may just believe her.

The Man Behind the WAC Clearinghouse: Mike Palmquist

CAROL RUTZ

First, the disclaimer: *The WAC Journal,* among many other resources devoted to WAC, is housed on The WAC Clearinghouse, a site hosted by Colorado State University: http://wac.colostate.edu/. We are delighted to be available to readers through that link in addition to subscription. So what is this site, and how did it find its way to the web?

The answer to that question requires a narrative about the site's founder and chief maintainer, Mike Palmquist, currently Associate Provost for Instructional Innovation at Colorado State University. This interview may dispel a great deal of ignorance among the WAC community about Mike and his derring-do as a higher-ed innovator—and perhaps raise more questions that could be pursued in another venue.

To begin, consider this recipe for a career path:

> Take one childhood in the Northern Minnesota woods, add a Merit Scholarship, awards in track and cross-country competition, and the initiative to edit an underground newspaper in high school.

> Add a liberal arts education at a small college, a post-graduate job as a VISTA volunteer and work as a free-lance writer.

> Stir in a doctorate in rhetoric that leads to an R1 job teaching writing, promoting technology in pedagogy, and advocating for imaginative administration.

> Cook at high heat for a few years.

> Remove (using heat-resistant mitts) and admire the result: a career that includes the WAC Clearinghouse and multiple awards for teaching and publications based on strong research on technology and assessment, as well as tireless work on faculty development and important student outcomes, including retention.

Clearly, Mike's current administrative responsibilities were divinely ordained. Or maybe not.

Fortunately, I have had a chance to ask Mike about his origins and career, and I owe him thanks for his willingness to exchange correspondence as well as for a dandy deli lunch in Tampa during the 2015 CCCC convention.

Carol Rutz: I will begin with an apology for taking so long in this interview series to approach you. You are, after all, the founding editor and nurturing parent of The WAC Clearinghouse: http://wac.colostate.edu/. I will ask later how that important project began, but first: how did WAC become important to you?

Mike Palmquist: WAC was something I became aware of in the mid-1980s as a graduate student at Carnegie Mellon. I had the good fortune to take a seminar on WAC and WID from Richard Young. We focused on a wide range of issues, including technology. He and Christine Neuwirth had recently submitted a funding proposal to the Buhl Foundation for a distributed, technology-based writing community that, had it been funded, would have led to the first OWL. It's pretty interesting to look at how they were configuring what would have been a social network built around writers sharing their expertise with less-experienced writers through commenting tools, chat, and access to network-based resources. This was long before the web, but Carnegie Mellon had a robust network that allowed for easy sharing of files and access to some fairly interesting writing tools. In Richard's seminar, we covered most of the major work in the field up to that time and I came out of it with a fairly good familiarity with the issues—at least theoretically.

CR: So are you saying that you learned about writing in various disciplinary contexts among researchers rather than through other means—e.g., personal interaction with faculty outside of the humanities?

MP: I hadn't thought about that until you asked it, but I think that's right. I was completely unfamiliar with writing studies when I went to graduate school. I'd worked as a professional writer for a few years and thought that was going well—right up to the point where my wife said, "Let's go to graduate school." We ended up at Carnegie Mellon on the basis of a recommendation from some faculty at the University of Minnesota, where my wife had taken some courses. The faculty at Carnegie Mellon challenged just about every assumption I had about writing and what it means to be a writer. A big part of that was my exposure to WAC. Richard and Christine weren't running a WAC program, but they provided me with a theoretical framework that has continued to shape my thinking about how to work with faculty—and very importantly, with students—on WAC initiatives. For Richard, WAC was both an interesting problem and a way to connect with faculty from other institutions. He'd been working with Robert Morris College on their WAC initiative and had compiled a collection of writing activities that spanned several disciplines. (With Richard's permission, I ended up turning that into a small book that's now available on the Clearinghouse.) But since he hadn't established a WAC program at Carnegie Mellon, my early exposure to WAC was very much a theoretical experience.

After I completed my degree, I found myself in meetings at Colorado State with Kate Kiefer, Dawn Rodrigues, and Don Zimmerman (a colleague from our technical communications program). Kate and Dawn had been involved in a decade-long effort to establish a WAC program at Colorado State. Unfortunately, while the faculty members who had become engaged in the program were enthusiastic, the number of participants was quite low (about twenty people from a faculty of one thousand). Dawn and Don had been approached by the dean of engineering about improving student writing and speaking skills. We used that invitation as an opportunity to seek funding for a more robust program. We ended up getting a large state grant that led to a network-supported program that combined some of Richard Young's and Christine Neuwirth's ideas with ideas that Kate and Dawn had been pursuing for several years. I added a focus on hypertext/hypermedia and we ended up, over the next few years, creating resources that students could consult through the network (guides to writing particular genres, videos that helped students prepare speeches and presentations, online tutorials, and tools that allowed writers to share their work with and get feedback from consultants in our writing center).

CR: That effort must have required considerable IT infrastructure. Did the grant support equipment and staff for the program?

MP: It did. We ended up hiring a full-time programmer and spent a lot of money on computers, software, video cameras, and so on. Initially, we were setting up our program on individual computers, so we weren't using anything that even remotely resembled a server.

CR: Your program seems much more attuned to students than mine at Carleton, for example, which began with an institutional recognition that students were assigned writing widely, but writing instruction was largely missing.

MP: One of the big changes for us was shifting from a top-down approach to WAC (the then-standard train-the-teachers model in which WAC specialists focused their efforts on helping faculty members get ready to teach writing and speaking) to a mixed model in which we provided support not only to faculty but also to students. We called it an integrated model since we were looking at both top-down and bottom-up (writing-center-based) models. We had found, through about a year of studies of students and faculty at our research-intensive university, that our colleagues in other disciplines were resistant to the idea of introducing activities that would increase the amount of time they were putting into their courses. Given the rewards structure in place, which privileged funded research and publication, that was understandable. Our goal was to reduce the barrier to adopting WAC practices by providing resources directly to students. We thought that if we could reduce the time commitment required to assign and respond to student writing from, say, forty hours to twenty hours over the course of the semester, we might see higher levels of faculty involvement.

CR: That was a practical and humane idea. What came of it?

MP: The good news was that we saw higher faculty involvement in WAC. We ended up growing our writing center (we characterized the "new" writing center as "the visible face of writing on our campus") and increasing student visits to it fairly substantially. The writing center consultants spent a fair amount of time running workshops for student writers. And faculty members used the resources we'd made available to support writing in their classes. It wasn't perfect, but it was a major improvement over the program that had been running through the 1980s.

CR: And what led to the Clearinghouse?

MP: In 1996, we had configured about four hundred or so computers on campus to use our "Online Writing Center." It was getting tedious to update everything manually on a regular basis. We recognized that the web (which was still quite new then) could help us distribute our materials far more easily and widely. The only downside was that the web was pretty primitive and we'd lose a lot of the media elements (video, audio, and some interactive content) if we moved to the web. But we also thought it would eventually catch up. So we moved the Online Writing Center to the web.

Shortly after that, it occurred to me that we could also offer resources to our faculty via the web. It took me about three minutes to realize (duh) that anything we put on the web would be accessible to everyone. There were already some good websites focused on WAC at that time, including the Northern Illinois site and the Language and Learning Across the Curriculum site. I didn't want to duplicate what they were doing, so I looked for other ways to design the site.

CR: You were remarkably prescient.

MP: I suspect it was one of those fortunate insights that changes a career—or perhaps I was just in a good place and working with the right people. In any event, at the CCCC convention in 1997, I talked about the idea of establishing the WAC Clearinghouse with Christine Hult from Utah State and Bill Condon from Washington State. They agreed to join the project and we recruited a small group of folks who helped plan the site. By fall 1997, we had a website up and running. There's a fairly clear history of this on the Clearinghouse at http://wac.colostate.edu/about/history.cfm. We had some early problems keeping people involved in the project, largely because the folks in English departments who were running annual performance reviews didn't know what to make of this kind of work. I think a lot of them thought that creating web-based resources was kind of a frivolous activity.

CR: No doubt—fortunately, you and your colleagues have outlasted that attitude. Throughout, I assume you have tallied the traffic on the site. Which pages are accessed most often? The journals? Individual WAC programs? Other links?

MP: The books and journals see the most traffic. We get quite a bit of traffic on our specialized resources, too. The bibliography that pulls from the CompPile database gets visited quite often; so do the L2 Writers and Writing Fellows pages. One of the most visited parts of the site is Kate Kiefer's introduction to WAC. She and I have revised that, and we should be putting the new version up soon. She really put a lot of time and effort (and a great deal of hard-won experience) into that resource.

CR: WAC is often characterized as a faculty development program that brings faculty from all disciplines into dialogue with writing pedagogy and assessment. Does that understanding have anything to do with your current post at CSU as Associate Provost for Instructional Innovation?

MP: I think so. My work with WAC and, more generally, the university composition program, put me into discussions with the provost's office pretty early in my career. That brought me into conversations that I might not otherwise have been invited to join.

In terms of my approach to supporting innovation in teaching and learning, WAC has been essential. I've learned about resistance to innovation. I've learned about the complex challenges posed by the rewards structures in place at my own and similar institutions. I've learned that change requires a great deal of patience and a great deal of clarity, particularly clarity about the benefits of putting the necessary time into making change—and that's true both for myself and for my colleagues at the university. And I've learned that you need to assess outcomes carefully and wisely—there's nothing worse than assessment strictly for the sake of assessment.

CR: No kidding. People do not appreciate assessments that waste their time, but they do appreciate findings that help them make constructive changes. What else are you learning?

MP: One of the more interesting things has been the parallel between resistance to using writing in classes and resistance to using technology—even in the face of faculty recognition that the wise use of writing or technology can lead to improvements in student learning and success. And that extends to shifting to more active forms of teaching and learning in our courses. We're focusing right now on active learning, increased interaction among students and faculty, and, as a way to support those two focuses, technology-enhanced learning. Over the past few years, I've been learning a great deal about the role of technology in supporting innovation. My work in computers and writing has been extremely influential in the development of my thinking about both WAC program design and instructional innovation in a wider sense. It probably seems like a more natural fit now than it did in the early to mid-1990s. Certainly, a few decades ago, there wasn't a great deal of overlap between technology, WAC, and general improvements to teaching and learning. Now, it makes more sense to think about the connections among these areas.

CR: You are a graduate of St. Olaf College, the cross-town rival of my employer, Carleton College, both in tiny Northfield, MN. Tell The WAC Journal readers a bit about your Minnesota experience.

MP: I grew up on the Mesabi Iron Range in northern Minnesota, a working-class area that draws most of its income from mining, lumbering, and tourism (I think there are a dozen lakes within a ten-mile radius of our house). My family (my parents, four brothers, and two sisters) and I lived a fairly rustic life on forty acres several miles north of the nearest small town, Chisholm. We heated our house with wood, grew a lot of our own food, gathered a lot of berries and nuts (who knew that hazelnuts were anything special—they literally grew on trees all over our forty acres), and raised hogs for the meat. It was a good life, but I was pretty clueless about everything from college to athletics.

Fortunately, I ended up becoming a fairly successful distance runner and was recruited by a number of colleges in the Midwest—except for the one place I would have gone to in a minute, the University of Minnesota. Had their track coach ever called me, I would have enrolled immediately, but he pretty much ignored me. (I got my revenge over the next four years, when I beat most of their runners in various meets.) Worse, I'd qualified for a National Merit Scholarship and sent my application to the University of Minnesota, but I didn't hear anything from their admissions office either. Anyway, one night, while I was chopping wood before dinner, I looked up at the pines around our house and the stars above them and thought, "There's no way I can move to a big city like Minneapolis or St. Paul." I decided at that moment to attend St. Olaf, largely because I'd been impressed with the quality of their recruiting materials and because, unlike the University of Minnesota, they'd offered me a great financial aid package. They gave me a full ride for academics and need (it helped immensely that my dad was out of work after breaking his leg—for the second time—while working as a lumberjack). I ended up getting a great education there. It was a pretty amazing experience, although somewhat challenging at times, given the rivalry between the Norwegians and the Swedes and the failure of my parents to become Lutherans.

CR: One of St. Olaf's signature programs, now defunct, alas, was the Paracollege, which encouraged special majors and attentive mentoring. You told me you participated in that program. Tell us about your experience.

MP: I went to St. Olaf with the intention of becoming the editor of a small-town newspaper. Along the way, I double-majored in English and political science, thinking they'd help me with writing and practical politics. But my English major had almost nothing to do with writing (except, as I recall, writing papers that used New Criticism to explore literature) and my political science major had nothing to do with practical politics (did I not say I was naïve?), so I designed a major in writing through the Paracollege. The Paracollege was one of the experimental initiatives that sprung up in a number of small colleges during the 1960s. It was based on the Oxford-Cambridge tutorial model and allowed me to take courses on a one-on-one basis with a faculty member. In fact, one of my Paracollege courses, which focused on designing publications, involved two faculty members. It was an incredible experience. My advisor, Paul Kirchner, who has since passed away, made me write a paper every week and then read it aloud to him while he drank his coffee and smoked his cigarettes (a perfect setting for a distance runner). He kindled my interest in rhetoric. I recall reading several of the Platonic dialogues and having some wonderful discussions about them. As part of my work in the Paracollege, I wrote a novel and explored everything from poetry to journalism. I was disappointed when they shut down the program a few years ago.

CR: Would you like to say something about motorcycles? For example, there must be a connection between helmeted, leather-clad cyclists and WAC. Help us out.

MP: I'm sure there is. No doubt it's the mindfulness required to stay upright for long periods of time while being ever watchful for distractions, diversions, and roadblocks. It's also connected, I think, to the need for escape. I started riding while I was working as a VISTA volunteer with the Community Design Center in Minneapolis. I was a community organizer working on urban gentrification issues in a neighborhood in St. Paul. I couldn't afford a car (the stipend was eighty dollars per week with no benefits), so I was taking the bus, and most of the time I was spending about two hours getting back and forth. One of my younger brothers, who was serving in the military in Germany then, suggested that I borrow his motorcycle. I was hooked after a few weeks of riding and have been riding ever since. I usually get at least one long ride in each summer, sometimes en route to the IWAC or C&W conferences. Last summer, I rode Route 66 with another brother (four of the five of us ride, although one rode a little too aggressively and has chosen to retire after a near-death experience). It was a great time and we're planning to head north to Glacier this year.

But I don't wear leather. Instead, I wear ballistic nylon and Kevlar and a bright yellow helmet. I saw a study of fatal motorcycle accidents sometime back in the 1990s that noted that none of the fatalities involved people wearing yellow helmets. I wear the most obnoxious yellow helmet available. Even Harley riders shy away when they see me coming. Come to think of it, I think a lot of department chairs do that, too, whenever they think I'm coming to talk with them about using writing in their courses. So, yes, I'm sure there's a connection between motorcycling and WAC.

CR: Well said! I'm going to start wearing my screaming yellow bicycle helmet to faculty meetings as sort of a WAC emblem. Thanks so much, Mike.

Contributors

Caitlin Holmes is a Term Assistant Professor of English at George Mason University. Her research interests include undergraduate research publication, online course development, editing practices, and writing pedagogy more broadly.

Mary Hedengren is a postdoctoral fellow at the University of Texas at Austin where she serves as Graduate Writing Coordinator for the University Writing Center. Her research focuses on the development of emerging identities, especially within the academy. Her work has appeared in *KB Journal*, *Present Tense*, *Praxis* and is forthcoming in *Pedagogy*.

Sherry Lee Linkon is Professor of English and Faculty Director of Writing Curriculum Initiatives at Georgetown University. She is active in scholarship of teaching and learning, and in 2003 was named the Ohio Professor of the Year. Along with her work on teaching and learning in the humanities, she does research on deindustrialization and working-class culture. She is the author or editor of six books, including *Literary Learning: Teaching in the English Major* (Indiana 2011), *Steeltown USA: Work and Memory in Youngstown* (Kansas, 2002, with John Russo), and *Teaching Working Class* (Massachusetts 1999).

Matthew Pavesich is Associate Teaching Professor of English and Associate Director of the Writing Program at Georgetown University. He teaches first-year writing, and undergraduate and graduate courses in rhetoric and composition pedagogy. His current project, DC/Adapters (dcadapters.org), traces a local material and rhetorical network, the first publication about which appeared in *Technoculture* in 2014.

Carol Rutz directs the writing program at Carleton College in Northfield, Minnesota. Her work includes teaching writing courses for several departments and working with the WAC faculty on assessment and faculty development. Recent research has involved seeking evidence that faculty development programs affect student learning as well as the teaching practices of individual faculty.

Katherine Schaefer is a Lecturer in the Writing, Speaking, and Argument Program at the University of Rochester. Originally trained as an RNA biochemist, she later switched to immunology, and after a fifteen-year career as an immunologist, became interested in teaching writing in the sciences. She currently teaches both freshman composition and professional communication and writing courses in Biology. In addition, she serves as a WID specialist and coordinates the Writing Workshop Program, which supports professors who include writing instruction in their discipline-specific courses. Her current research interests include (1) developing additional approaches to teaching genre and (2) understanding how interactions between teachers in team-taught science courses affect student learning. This is her first publication relating to writing instruction.

Erika Scheurer is Associate Professor of English and Director of Writing Across the Curriculum at the University of Saint Thomas in Saint Paul, Minnesota. For many years she also served as Coordinator of the Academic Development Program for at-risk students. Her scholarship spans the fields of literature and composition, with presentations and publications on Emily Dickinson, voice theory and pedagogy, basic writing, and, more recently, writing across the curriculum. Current research includes continued work on faculty perspectives on "coverage" through case studies as well as explorations of the intersections of writing pedagogy and mindfulness.

Denise Ann Vrchota is an assistant professor in the Communication Studies Program, Department of English at Iowa State University. Her research area is communication in the disciplines. She consults with faculty outside of the communication discipline, helping them integrate communication activities into their classes. She is the co-author of a public speaking textbook, *Everyday Public Speaking*. With David R. Russell, she co-authored an article that appeared in an earlier issue of *The WAC Journal*. She has also published in *Communication Education* and the *Journal of Food Science Education*.

How to Subscribe

The WAC Journal is published annually in print by Parlor Press and Clemson University. Digital copies of the journal are simultaneously published at The WAC Clearinghouse in PDF format for free download. Print subscriptions support the ongoing publication of the journal and make it possible to offer digital copies as open access. Subscription rates: One year: $25; Three years: $65; Five years: $95. You can subscribe to *The WAC Journal* and pay securely by credit card or PayPal at the Parlor Press website: http://www.parlorpress.com/wacjournal. Or you can send your name, email address, and mailing address along with a check (payable to Parlor Press) to

> Parlor Press
> 3015 Brackenberry Drive
> Anderson SC 29621
> Email: sales@parlorpress.com

Pricing

One year: $25 | Three years: $65 | Five years: $95

Publish in The WAC Journal

The editorial board of The WAC Journal seeks WAC-related articles from across the country. Our national review board welcomes inquiries, proposals, and 3,000 to 6,000 word articles on WAC-related topics, including the following:

- WAC Techniques and Applications
- WAC Program Strategies
- WAC and WID
- WAC and Writing Centers
- Interviews and Reviews

Proposals and articles outside these categories will also be considered. Any discipline-standard documentation style (MLA, APA, etc.) is acceptable, but please follow such guidelines carefully. Submissions are managed initially via Submittable (https://parlor-press.submittable.com/submit) and then via email. For general inquiries, contact Lea Anna Cardwell, the managing editor, via email (wacjournal@parlorpress.com). The WAC Journal is an open-access, blind, peer-viewed journal published annually by Clemson University, Parlor Press, and the WAC Clearinghouse. It is available in print through Parlor Press and online in open-access format at the WAC Clearinghouse.

PARLOR PRESS
EQUIPMENT FOR LIVING

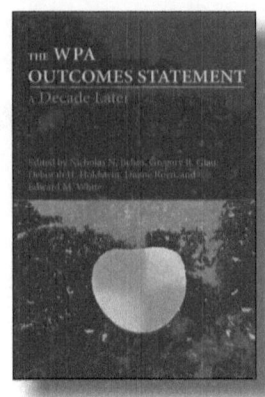

Congratulations to These Award Winners & WPA Scholars!

The WPA Outcomes Statement—A Decade Later
Edited by Nicholas N. Behm, Gregory R. Glau, Deborah H. Holdstein, Duane Roen, and Edward M. White
Winner of the Best Book Award, Council of Writing Program Adminstrators (July, 2015)

GenAdmin: Theorizing WPA Identities in the Twenty-First Century
Colin Charlton, Jonikka Charlton, Tarez Samra Graban, Kathleen J. Ryan, & Amy Ferdinandt Stolley
Winner of the Best Book Award, Council of Writing Program Adminstrators (July, 2014)

Mics, Cameras, Symbolic Action: Audio-Visual Rhetoric for Writing Teachers
Bump Halbritter
Winner of the Distinguished Book Award from *Computers and Composition* (May, 2014)

New Releases

First-Year Composition: From Theory to Practice
Edited by Deborah Coxwell-Teague & Ronald F. Lunsford. 420 pages.

Twelve of the leading theorists in composition studies answer, in their own voices, the key question about what they hope to accomplish in a first-year composition course. Each chapter includes sample syllabi.

A Rhetoric for Writing Program Administrators
Edited by Rita Malenczyk. 471 pages.

Thirty-two contributors delineate the major issues and questions in the field of writing program administration and provide readers new to the field with theoretical lenses through which to view major issues and questions.

www.parlorpress.com

www.ingramcontent.com/pod-product-compliance
Lightning Source LLC
Chambersburg PA
CBHW030406170426
43202CB00010B/1507